How to
Self-Publish
for under
$100

The Step-by-Step Handbook to Publishing Your Book Without Breaking the Bank

Cinquanta Cox-Smith

For permission requests, please contact the publisher at:
Mango Publishing Group
2850 Douglas Road, 3rd Floor
Coral Gables, FL 33134 USA
info@mango.bz

For special orders, quantity sales, course adoptions and corporate sales, please email the publisher at sales@mango.bz.

For trade and wholesale sales, please contact Ingram Publisher Services at customer.service@ingramcontent.com or +1.800.509.4887.

How to Self-Publish for Under $100
ISBN: 978-1-63353-554-1
Printed in the United States of America

This book is dedicated to my husband Shawn and my kids Kyree and Sharye. The sacrifices I needed to make while preparing for this release were not easy. Thank you all for being supportive, your patience with my mood swings, and letting me sometimes lock myself in the room to finish a daily word count. I am excited to celebrate this journey with you all. I love you all more than I love string cheese.

To Mom, Dad, and Sister. Thank you for being my support system.

I want to send a special dedication to all the dreamers and aspiring content creators who have been following my journey. Every inch of knowledge that I could provide is in this book. This one is for YOU. To my YouTube Subscribers, my social media followers, and my blog readers: I hope you will continue to support me as we continue inspiring everyone to live their dreams.

Table of Contents

// Introduction

Ever had a goal that you thought was out of reach, but you somehow ended up living that dream? Well, that's pretty much how I became an Amazon Best Selling Author. I'm Cinquanta, and I have self-published twelve books and created a residual income by following my dreams. I'm not here to tell you how easy it is or that you can magically have a book written in thirty days and become a millionaire. Nope, I want to save you the agony of getting your hopes up only to be let down by the harsh reality of self-publishing. I do want to be able to show you how to self-publish on a very tight budget. You can still create something beautiful without a lot of money. Most authors who have never written anything in their lives start with a small income. You will have to be committed and sacrifice a few things to get your project off the ground, but the valuable information I will share with you could save you from spending hundreds of dollars that you won't make back.

My friend Diane can tell you a thing are two about self-publishing:

It's been six months since I published my first book on Amazon. I thought I'd be well on the way to notoriety, infamy and gazillionaire status (also known as being able to quit my day job) by now. I thought I would write my books, publish them, and the dollars would start rolling in. I would bask in the glory of being an author, with actual published books (well, electronic ones anyway,) and I'd be invited to conferences and summits and to guest present at seminars and workshops and on radio shows, and everyone in the entire world would be keen to hear what I had to say about my books and this self-publishing lark.

Nothing could be further from the truth. I am but an insignificant and powerless grain of sand waiting to be washed away into oblivion by the relentless Amazon tide.

It's quite depressing, because I know I can write, and I know I write well, and I know that readers love what I write, but standing out in an extremely crowded marketplace without spending a gazillion dollars on promotion is quite tricky. No one tells you about that. Well, they probably do, but as humans we often won't do it, this information has been blocked out and buried, not least by me.

So this post is, in part, about addressing the dearth of information about what it's really like to self-publish, because according to practically everyone, Amazon is a goldmine. Except it isn't, not in my experience anyway. And it's because I've approached it the wrong way and by the wrong way, I mean being clueless about it all.

1. Make sure you do your research
2. Don't skip the launch of your book
3. Don't rely on the first book of a series to sell the rest
4. Misunderstanding the review process
5. Get your calls to action right
6. Don't skimp on promotion

I thought self-publishing would be easier than it is. And by easier, I mean not as hard to get traction and a foothold in the market. Six months in, I thought I'd be much further advanced than I am. Granted, I've learned a lot, and I can use this knowledge with any subsequent books I release, BUT I can't help feeling that I've lost momentum in the six months I've spent wandering dazed and confused around the Amazon wasteland.

If I had my time again, I would have done a lot more research about what is required to be a successful author on Kindle; but hopefully, after reading this post, you'll go in the direction I should have gone.

Instead, I got caught up with the exciting idea that I
was an author, even if I was a self-published one...

-Diane
www.dianelee.com.au/

You see, we all get in over our heads, and there are probably
tons of books that will tell you how to be a best-seller, or how
to write a book in seven days. You know what they leave out:
trusting others with your ideas and budget. I'm all for getting
help, but what happens when business deals go wrong?
These are the stories I want you to hear before you take this
journey. I want you to know that the steps I provide for you
are tried and true. I've made mistakes myself, and my fellow
self-published authors are sharing their stories to let you
know they have also made mistakes and failed attempts.

My best piece of advice comes from my own failed experience. When working to promote one of my books, I hired a social media/public relations firm to help with promotions. We did have a signed contract, and things were going smoothly for the first several months, after which things started to degrade. Posts and emails would be sent with my signature without approval or with misspellings or information I wasn't looking to share. The biggest fail came when I got a bill for several hundred dollars more than I had budgeted for graphics, because the individual kept outsourcing the graphic and promotional work without approval. We tried to reach out and settle the difference, but each time I was referred to the bill, and the graphic company had several overdue statements that I was not aware off. Everything has been settled now, and that relationship has unfortunately been terminated. It was a tough and expensive lesson to learn, but now I know more about business, contracts, and staying on top of vendors who have spending control.

-TS Krupa

When we have this vision of being an Author, we do some research, but reading information without actually trying something leaves a large gray area for the what ifs.

Here's another fail story from one of my fellow authors:

I knew nothing about self-publishing when I decided to book this blog and publish it as the Love & Other Stuff series. Nothing. Nada. Zip. Actually, that's not true. I knew nothing about self-publishing (other than I'm quite IT savvy so how hard could it be?) and a bit about publishing (as in I've been rejected by both major and minor publishers alike, and I read published books). What I did know was that I wanted to publish, and more importantly, with the tools that are currently available, could publish. And publish I did: two books down and four more to go, plus an infinite number of possibilities for Love & Other Stuff. And a whole lot of other writing and publishing projects demanding my attention.

The good thing about publishing one book, though, is that when you start the second, you know more than you did when you began this crazy adventure and the whole process gets easier. From designing the cover, to collating my content, to editing, to understanding e-book file types, to uploading my book, to marketing, I'm much more efficient and confident. And much less scared.

(Actually, if anyone tells you that self-publishing isn't a scary kind of caper to be involved in, they're either lying or stupid or both. It's all kinds of scary. You have your work— you!– right out there with no protection, no safe cover, no camouflage, waiting to be judged by readers. And judged you will be. From people disliking your cover and your structure and your pacing and your font and your editorial choices to schadenfreude over a missed typo and derision and/or disappointment over not doing a print run—you will be judged! Lucky for me, I've been blogging for a while, so my hide is reasonably tough. For those of you hitting the publish button for the first time, well, I feel your pain. And anguish. And vulnerability.)

Part of my journey included incorporating the learnings of other self-publishers who had gone before me, and who generously shared their own experiences via their books and blogs. These included the dreaded tax requirements of the IRS when sorting out Amazon and Smashwords payments for non-U.S. residents, to Kindle's blurred cover issues, to Amazon's missing reviews, to setting up my MailChimp opt-in on my blog.

- Lilly Shore

Does it make it easier for you when someone outlines all her fails for you? I want you to really read these stories and understand that self-publishing is worth it when things start to roll. I want you to understand that this is a decision that will change the way you think. I don't want you to just take my word for it, and that's why I have included these self-publishing fail stories; the information I will provide for you to create your book within your budget will save you the hundreds of dollars that these authors have lost.

"Self-publishing is so easy."

"My friend is making so much money as a self-published writer."

"Self-publishing means you make all the money."

Does this sound familiar? These are comments I heard many times when I was debating whether to self-publish.

I'm an Australian romance writer and had been writing and learning my craft for nine years before I made the momentous decision to self-publish. Had I known how hard it would be, I may not have ventured into this demanding and difficult world.

Yes, it turns out self-publishing is hard. Hard, as in really, really hard. All those authors who "seem" to be making money so easily are actually working hard. And because I listened to this so called great advice, I made mistakes, a lot of mistakes.

Let's zip back to July 2015 when I put my debut novel, Falling for Mr. Wrong, on Amazon, Barnes, and Noble, iTunes, and Kobo. Okay, let's celebrate, woo hoo, as I'm now a published author. But did I make any sales? Not much. A few friends kindly bought my book, but really, it just languished there.

On Amazon, it started with a good placing and then it dropped and dropped some more, till it became buried in the hundreds of thousands of Kindle paid books where it was unlikely to be seen again.

Think about it. Most readers will look at the top one hundred to two hundred books to buy before they do something else. They're not going to find you at 798,123!!!!

The few sales I had from friends and family helped, but there was no way I was even close to recovering the cost of editing, formatting, and the cover (approximately $1000).

My self-publishing fails:

Fail #1 – listening to the wrong people and believing that self-publishing would make me a well-known author. Fail!

Fail #2 - try before outlaying a wad of cash. I was recommended an editor, so I gave her four books to edit. Turned out, she wasn't the editor for me. Nice person, but not the editor I needed. This mistake cost $2000!!! (I had to re-edit those four books with a different editor.)

Fail #3 – work with people who respect you and your deadlines. I worked with a cover artist recommended to me. Not only did she turn out to be super expensive, but she stopped answering emails, didn't do the job, and I almost missed a deadline. A mistake that cost $150 and an almost missed deadline.

Fail #4 – expecting your writing friends and colleagues in the industry will support you like you supported them. There is no cost to this except for hurt feelings and a wonder why your friends are not there for you.

Fail #5 – paying way too much for promotions. Companies are there to make money and not sell your book. Don't be sucked in by their spiel. They don't care how many books you sell once you've paid to be a part of their promo. This mistake cost me $300.

Sure, anyone can put a book on Amazon. You can even save costs by doing the editing, formatting, and cover yourself. What now? Who's going to buy your book? Most likely no one.

Some writers try some unethical practices to get their Amazon ranking higher. However, I'm not focusing on that, because my advice is for writers who are genuinely interested in selling a quality book/s.

To be a successful self-published writer, you have to do more than write. Even a well-written book will get buried in all the other books on Amazon, iTunes, Kobo, and B&N, unless you treat it as a business.

Look at my fun romance, Falling for Mr. Wrong. It had been professionally edited, formatted, and had a beautiful cover. Why weren't readers snapping it up? It's a good read, a quality romance. The great reviews I've received confirm that.

It's not being snapped up because there are way too many great books on Amazon. It's a massive site, and like the other online retailers, it's not easy for readers to find and buy your book unless they are specifically searching for you.

There is no one place to find information on how to self-publish. You may get snippets of information, but it's not easy, as each country has different procedures.

My advice for writers interested in self-publishing is:

1. Accept you need to outlay money if you want a quality book.
2. Your friends and family may not buy your book, nor leave a review for you.
3. There's no quick rich scheme to self-publishing.
4. Successful self-published authors treat it as a business.
5. Self-publishing is hard.
6. Self-publishing is hard (yes, I did repeat it, because it is).

It's not all doom and gloom—you can do well, but it takes time, money, and a lot of work. You need to be realistic about the effort required.

The keys to being a successfully self-published writer are:

1. You have a quality book.
2. Your book is professionally edited, formatted, and with a decent cover.
3. You have a good-sized subscriber list and email them one to two times a month.
4. You're writing the next book.
5. You promote your books through paid and unpaid promotions.

6. You work collaboratively with other writers.

7. You are active on social media.

By December 2016, I will have seven books available in both print and e-book format. My sales rankings are good, I have excellent reviews on all my books, and I have a subscriber list in the thousands. All of this was achieved in less than eighteen months.

How did I do this? There is no simple answer, but the big thing I did was to seek advice and learn from experts.

Yes, there are very successful authors out there who generously share their advice... for a cost. As they should. They give hours of assistance in understanding the online retailers, advising how to promote your book, appreciating the complexities of the self-publishing landscape, and tips on promotions.

If you're interested, check out Joanna Penn, Marie Force, Nick Stephenson, and Mark Dawson. There are plenty of others, but these are the writers who have not only helped, but also inspired my "overnight success" (which took ten years).

-Joanne Dannon

Now, that you've heard all of the terrible things that could happen when you don't have the proper guidance, I want to guide you through the self-publishing process for under $100. I have some great suggestions, tips, and tricks that will have you feeling like you've left the library. I want to give you information you can use right away. I get overwhelmed when I read how-to books; when you're just an average person trying to become an author, complicated tools and resources aren't helpful to beginners.

I want you to have this book be your bookmark, Google, Bible, your ultimate workbook. So, now that you know a little bit more about my mission and why I wrote this book, let's begin on your path to becoming a pretty darn good self-published author.

/ Legal Notes

damage, or disruption caused by errors or omissions, whether such errors or omissions result from negligence, accident, or any other cause.

It should be noted that there is no magic trick that will make you a *New York Times* best-seller.

Following the advice in this book could help you through the writing process. On the other hand, it may not, and you could find yourself back at square one. So, regardless of the claim I just made—and the claims I made on the cover, back cover, and throughout this book—I make no claims. Use my advice and methods at your own risk. Don't blame me or the publisher for anything that does not get fixed trying to implement the advice in this book. If things work out well for you, please write a long 5-star review on Amazon about how much my advice and methods helped you. Now that we've cleared that up, let's get on with *How to Self-Publish for Under $100.*

Chapter 1: Find Your Purpose

// Chapter 1: Find Your Purpose

Purpose:
The reason you are creating or completing something to exist.

By now, if you have picked up this book, you have an interest in writing. You either have something written already, or you're still researching your genre. There are so many things you can write about, and there are so many books out in the world today. Self-publishing has become a very big and lucrative business.

When I first started writing it was my sixth grade teacher, Mrs. Delaney, who made writing an exciting part of school for me. I remember every day I looked forward to her English class. She made learning about haikus, similes, assonance, metaphors, and onomatopoeias a great experience. I had never been that ecstatic to learn and embrace them like I was when we started to learn about poetry.

I started small with poems, and by high school, it took on a life of its own. I had a binder with plastic sleeves full of poems I had written. Some were poems about being happy, and others were about love. I had kind of experienced my first heartbreak in middle school. I had over one hundred poems in this binder, and I wouldn't let anyone read it. I was protective about my work. Maybe I was just shy to have someone criticize something I wrote.

By college, I would get rave reviews on my essay papers and how I was able to tell stories. I could take a simple topic and create a vivid picture for my reader. I really loved this thing called writing.

It wasn't until my late twenties that I realized I was struggling with my purpose. I was trying all sorts of different entrepreneurial fields. I'm creative, but things weren't sticking. I started with t-shirts, hair, jewelry, cell phone cases, clutch purses, and lastly, skirts. There was no denying that I was very talented, but the substance was missing. These things didn't fulfill me. They would last for about six months at the most.

I started talking to my best friend, and I told her we should write a book, either together or just write. We had been friends since seventh grade, and we had a lifetime of stories to tell. We could easily do this for the rest of our lives. Things didn't go as a planned with our joint book. But I never stopped writing. I continued to write. It was on computer paper, and it was just random thoughts and characters. I had no prior knowledge of being an author, but that didn't stop me.

Fast forward to October 2014. I had to pick up my life and move away to Kansas. My whole life got uprooted, and me and my family took the long trip from Georgia to the plains. I had to leave my full-time and part-time job where I was comfortable. That's just a sacrifice that comes with a military family, though. In my quest to Kansas, I thought about things, like where I would work and what I would do. Most of all, I continued to write. I thought about my legacy. Where do I want to leave a mark? What is my purpose?

All along it was right in front of me. I researched information after I read about a YouTuber who had self-published her own book. I was all over the Internet now, searching for more and more information on how I could self-publish the book I'd been working on.

Once I felt like I knew enough to get me by, I hit the publish button. I had published my first book. Journeys of the Heart. I barely told anyone. I was still shocked myself. When I searched for it and I found it on Amazon was when I noticed that I had indeed found my purpose.

That book has gone on to sell over five hundred copies with a mediocre cover, horrible editing, and unflattering formatting. I relaunched the book after a year and went on to sell over one thousand copies total. My relaunch included editing, a professional cover, and a well-formatted book.

Because people believed in me, I persevered. My first failed attempt at self-publishing was still successful. I feel my story was good, so my readers were intrigued.

- Cinquanta Cox-Smith

Finding your purpose shouldn't be a marathon; you shouldn't have to participate in a scavenger hunt to find it. When things don't work for you, you should look at yourself. Are you blaming others for your shortcomings? Once you reevaluate your goals you need to find your way.

Getting out of your own way

- Stop being uncomfortable with your life choices
- It's okay to fail because at least you tried

- Procrastination only leads you farther away from your dream
- No one is going give you exactly what you want

Your Life Purpose

- Learn new skills that can help you be better
- Time Management for Life Purpose
- Research things you are good at
- Vision Board and Goal Setting

In order to find your purpose, you should be actively doing things. If you are at a standstill, this is where you need to pay close attention and follow the list. I want to go over a few examples of things that you can do to actively prepare yourself as an author.

Research. I know I say this a lot, but it is truly my number one piece of advice. I have to give you this type of information because it's not always in plain sight. You need to research numerous things about the genre you choose to write in.

Dialogue information, and how to create character outlines, are also important. A Google search is not always enough. Try going to a library to get an actual book that has years of history in it. The library is a very reliable source. You need to know things about creating location names and copyright laws.

Next, you should be doing whatever is set in your heart to do. If you are passionate about teaching content creators how to take their courses from online to an e-book, for example, you should find someone who you can possibly help to test out your skill.

Writing makes me happy, and it makes me excited. I love when I get inbox messages from people who tell me I've made a difference in their lives with my words. My heart melts. I try my best to write things that have meaning. I love fiction, but I feel that every story should have a lesson. Sometimes you have to go through the mud to get to the good part.

Knowing that you, in some way, shape, or form, have put your heart into your craft—and it's reflecting on your reviews that should make your heart smile.

Never think that your purpose is only ONE thing. You may think you are called to just do one thing in life, but really, you can have many gifts. If your gift can be spread out into three or more sources of income, your focus will then shift to all three of your purposes.

Don't believe that notion that you can only be one thing in life. Nope, you can certainly be more than one. Even if you don't know what those others things are yet, it's okay to try out options in new territories. Failure isn't defeat.

Being able to try new things can open your eyes to a bigger purpose than the one you thought you had.

Here is a task that I want you to complete to help you find your purpose. Freewriting is what opens your mind and your heart. It doesn't have to be grammatically correct or even make sense.

1. Take out a sheet of paper
2. At the top write the word purpose
3. Write any word or thought that may come to your mind
4. Repeat this step until you have an aha moment (cry, laugh, or smile)

Once you find out what your purpose is—and again it maybe more than the one—you need to start your new journey of living in your purpose.

/ How to start living in your purpose

When you start to feel that there isn't an emptiness in your life, you have truly found your purpose and what makes you whole. I like to say living in your purpose makes you feel alive—it's like starting a new life. You will feel fulfilled and that your life has more meaning than it did before you started living in your purpose. Doing the work brings you more joy and no longer sucks the energy out of you. When you aren't living in your purpose, the things you are doing often suck you dry and everything tends to become negative, no matter how hard you to try to be positive. Doing something that you are destined to do sometimes wakes you out of your sleep because it lives deep inside of you.

No longer doubting yourself is a for sure way to know you are currently living in your purpose. All of the choices you make are done with confidence and pride. The worrying, insecurity, and old procrastination traits are gone out the window. You feel a sense of power knowing that the world will need you at your best, and that's what you will now strive to be. You have people who are looking for the service you provide and your income starts to increase. You have now experienced an overflow in the financial area of your life. You no longer feel the need to hide the creativity inside you that you were afraid to express. You can be your true self and share it with the world. You are now more patient when dealing with certain types of people, but you trust yourself enough to say no when you need to. The next steps in your life appear scary, but you trust your decisions more than ever.

One major way to know you are living in your purpose is that you no longer search or feel like you need approval from others. Your voice and courage are what matters to you. With those two things, you can conquer the world. You can now pitch your ideas and freely talk about the things you have created or written. Your characters are now a part of your life. You're fearless, and you feel alive.

I used to struggle with becoming so frustrated that things weren't working, but as soon as I started living in my purpose, everything that was meant for me came to light. The frustration vanished, and the opportunities were lined up at the door. Change. It's a word I used to be very afraid of, but I no longer fear change. I embrace it. Once you accept things that you cannot change, it will allow you to create a lifestyle that you love.

Your budget may be small, but once you find wiggle room, you will be able to eliminate the things that weren't necessary to invest in your vision or your dream. The struggle won't be real anymore, because you're living your life with passion and purpose.

We often feel like we are selling our souls for a few bucks when we are just in the figuring-it-out stage, but once you're living in your purpose, your income will fall into place. Others will believe in your gift when you start to believe in yourself. You no longer put your life on hold. You are truly living in your destiny. You owe it to yourself to live every day like your last. I wish I could paint you a picture of how amazing it feels to live in your purpose, but I have a pretty good feeling that you will be on the right track once you get past this chapter.

You will get to know what happiness feels like when you are living in your purpose. Living in your purpose your excitement and visions will keep you up at night. Getting random ideas in the middle of the night, while in the shower, and sometimes even when you're driving.

My purpose is creating magical stories that make you feel like you're a character in the book.

That's an example of living in your purpose by actively doing things.

// Chapter 2: Creating Original Content

Original:

Something that was created by one artist and it is not to be copied or imitated.

As a writer, creating original content can sometimes become a daunting task. You have an idea that you think is fresh and new, only to do a search and find out that it's been done before, or there is something fairly similar to your idea. I can tell you that it's possible to find something that's outside the box, and that's original. You just have to believe in yourself.

I feel that we should all surround ourselves with certain people that contribute to our thinking when it comes to creating content.

As a writer, there is no way you can read every book and synopsis in your genre to make sure you're not copying anyone's storyline. It would be impossible. When I start new a new story or a new series, there is always a few things that I do that can also help you with creating fresh new content. These few tips will help you dig deeper to find new ideas to write about.

/ 5 Content Creation Tips

• Speak from Experiences

Speak or write about something you have dealt with in your life. If you have a better solution to the problem, write about a character choosing the better option than you did. If you had an extremely hard break up, it would be easy to write with those emotions. A lot of times we create masterpieces from our failures. People love to know how you did something, and when you don't paint it all magical but include the struggles, they relate to you.

• Ask Your Audience

You can ask your friends what they like to read about. Social media is a good platform to also ask this question on. You can get advice on what genre people love to read. If you have a large audience who have opinions, this source will never go dry. It's refreshing to get inspiration from the people who you inspire.

• Set A Timer

Grab a timer and set it for thirty minutes. Get your pen and paper out and brainstorm until your timer goes off. If this doesn't work for you, take a walk, or even a long drive. I get great ideas in the shower—I've made sure I have a waterproof pad to capture my thoughts. Most people have smartphones which come equipped with an easy to use timer.

• Write It Down

You need to write it down as soon as you think of it, wherever you are. Once it's gone from your thoughts, you won't be able to remember it. I struggled with this step in the early stages of writing. Now I carry a notebook and pen with me at all times.

• Try It Out

If you are still scared about putting your work out there, try out Wattpad. It's a website where you can upload free stories and share them on your social media platforms. This helps you get comfortable with sharing and marketing your work. If your blog has great views, you can create free blog stories, too. This has recently been an amazing asset to my writing. Sharing a free short story has gained me new readers and new sales.

....

You need two types of people in your corner. Many people feel that writers never run out of ideas. I'm here to tell you we get stumped, and writer's block is real.

Everyone should have someone who can critique their writing. If you have a "yes man" or woman who constantly says they love everything you do, you need to find a new naysayer. You need someone who can critique your writing and also be able to tell you what's wrong with it. They need to understand your vision, but also give you a list of problems you may face with that idea.

You also need someone on your team who can read your writing and push you to the next level, someone who sees your storyline going farther. That person will help you dig deeper into scenes or character development. This person may be able to see parts or holes in your story that can be filled to make it complete.

I don't want you to look at these people as negative, because they are there to help you. We all need a little help, and we should never let our pride lead our careers. I get opinions, but I get them from someone I trust.

The reality is when we create something we become attached. Most of the time we are emotionally attached to our writing. I know there are people out there who write stories and then they never read them; the story was their emotions falling out of them onto paper. It's like therapy, and once it's written, the process of healing is over. Reading that emotional piece is like opening an old wound.

We don't want someone to give negative feedback because we may not be able to handle it. The truth is, we need it. I've written a little over ten books now. I have no reviews that are less than four stars on Amazon. (I also wrote a blog post called "No Bad Reviews.") I know I have areas in my writing that I can improve, but if my readers aren't giving me their honest, unfiltered reviews, how can I improve? I have people who send me private messages with their reviews and I appreciate that, but I never want anyone to spare my feelings because of how they think I will react. Being an author, this comes with your success. Not everyone will love what you do.

I think this is a good time to share a personal story on how I create my stories and what my process is.

So, freewriting is basically writing what comes to your mind without an outline that provides structure.
What would you think if I told you that many of my books or my short stories have been written without an outline, and sometimes I start a story without character names or location? I start with a plain canvas of just an idea. Then it turns itself into something I can't even explain. I wouldn't give you this advice and tell you this is how you should create your stories, but most of the time it works for me.

When people tell me that I usually leave my stories with amazing cliffhangers that leave them wanting more, I'm always thrilled. Verbally, my storytelling skills aren't that good, but give me a pen and paper, or let my fingers do the talking on the computer, and something magical happens. I can't explain it, but my thoughts just flow from my head into a story, and once it's done, it would make you feel that I've spent hours or months creating it.

My most-sold book was written in two days on my cell phone while I was at work. I had an idea, and I wanted to see if I could write in a different genre; the story was born. It was supposed to be just one story, and now it has turned into this wonderful short story series that's getting ready to end with book five.

I often go back and read my stories, adding more things to it. This is the freedom that I have because I decided on self-publishing. I can go back and add new angles or more description into a story that I may feel like is lacking in an area. I have complete control over my books, can access all of my stories, and change, delete, or add something whenever I need to. I can easily change my cover and relaunch my book with a different edition, which is something I've done with two of my books. As a self-published author, you are constantly learning what works for you when it comes to writing. You can use your reviews or your interactions with your readers to figure out what needs to be tweaked in your story.

. . . .

I want to go back and elaborate on the five creation tips I gave you. I don't want to just tell you what to do, but I want to give you ideas and great instructions to lay out what each tip means.

- Speak from Experiences

Depending on the genre, this could be the easiest step of them all. I know a lot of people have interesting, "small moment" stories about their life. You can even use a "remember that time" story. When I write my realistic fiction stories, I sometimes create a story from just a small moment in my life. It could be a memory from my childhood that I turn into a short story, or it could be a life changing moment in my life that I can use, exaggerating the event or the characters to turn it into a full novel. If you have friends or family members—who don't mind you using their life stories as a stepping stone—feel free to use a small moment from their story and turn it around. I love taking positive things from my life and changing it into a negative trait of a character. I do this because, just like in life, everything's not going to be sunshine and roses. When you create fiction stories, you have to show the good and the bad. Sometimes, stories you create are just a small part of your life and will reach someone in your audience differently. You want to create storylines that will make people laugh, cry, or feel mad, all at the same time. A big part of original content comes from your experiences.

- Ask Your Audience

Whether you're a content creator or a regular person with dreams of being a great writer, you have some type of audience. A blogger has its readers who come to her blog to read new content and leave comments. A vlogger has viewers who come to his channel to see his new content in video format. We have the social media mavens who are influencers for different brands. They all have one thing in common: they have a voice and people listen. My YouTube audience was the audience who helped me get the courage to publish my first book. They were also the first to purchase a copy. I now involve my audience in most of my new writing by giving sneak peeks on Facebook. If they love it and share it, I continue to write. If I don't get a lot of interaction, I know I need to tweak some things. For the new writer, I advise you to share snippets of your work in different Facebook groups, look for creative writing groups at your local library, and share it wherever you see fit. Your audience will give you the feedback you need, and they will also let you know what they like to read. I often ask people on my Facebook page questions like, "What are you reading? How many books have your read? What genre do you enjoy?"

- Set A Timer

This is pretty much like freewriting to me, but in a timeframe you set for yourself. It could be as simple as picking two to three topics or ideas that you want to write about, and then scheduling thirty minutes to write about each. You will find your winner by noticing when a subject has a larger word count than the others. You can set the same amount of time for all three, but when you end up with a higher word count for one, this is the idea or topic you need to focus on. It's obvious, because either you have more background with that idea or you're more connected to that topic. I can always tell the stories that I'm more passionate about because I finish them faster. When creating your content, sometimes procrastination can come into play. So, when I know that I am on a deadline, I also set a timer or create a schedule to be finished by. Not all deadlines will be met that you set for yourself. Things like this are flexible because life happens. I suggest you get used to pulling out that timer to get some good creative writing going.

• Write It Down

I cannot stress this enough for you, to write everything down. Every single idea, you have to write it down. I have at least ten journals. I have one in my purse, at work, at my desk, by my bed, and even in my car. I keep a pen or pencil on me so I can write whenever I feel the urge. Some of my ideas are a little farfetched, but to me, just writing down those ideas means I'm constantly creating and working. I may never use it, or I may need it down the road. Another way to know when your creative juices are flowing is, for a week, write down where you are when you come up with your best idea. Once you see the pattern, you need to make sure you have paper and a writing utensil nearby. Sometimes, looking at a picture or seeing a quote may spark an idea. I feel that when we constantly do the same thing over and over again, it may stall our creative juices. Try doing something out of your comfort zone, like going to a museum, listening to a live band play, or go the park. Doing at least one thing out of your normal routine can spark a vantage point for you to write from. With that pad and pen in your possession, you'll be ready to jot down some awesome content.

- Try it Out

This has to be the scariest part when it comes to your content. I get it. You're a new or fairly new author and, so far, you haven't gotten the reaction you want when it comes to your writing. I want you to reevaluate your process and try it out again. But this time someplace else. Sometimes certain areas aren't created for the type of content we want to share. I feel that the easier place to share and try out your content is on your blog. Have you created a following or an email list? This should be where you blast your work first. If you don't get the feedback there that you were looking for, then you need to try your next share-space. I would then take my talents to social media, and you can get creative there. You can share your writing or content in parts. Share a little at a time until you have your audience's attention. When they start to ask for more, share a little bit extra as a follow-up. It's a little harder on Twitter and Instagram. It's just perfect for Facebook. You can catch a pretty good flow with retweets and likes on Twitter when you constantly share your story. It has to start off really good and have a strong follow-up. These are just other examples of how you can try out your content.

....

I hope these ideas and tips have helped you gain a perspective on how to get started when it comes to creating original content.

I feel it's okay to also start numerous stories and blog posts. It's actually pretty helpful. Have material half-written or started blog posts are great for days when you feel like you've completed all your tasks and are ahead of schedule. Having unfinished blog posts are good for the days when you don't have content ready.

When you decide you want to self-publish, you should also do your research. Research is a big part of doing something on your own. You need to learn about copyright laws and publishing lingo. I suggest you research the subject or the storyline that you are getting ready to write about. It may help to look at book covers in the genre. I wouldn't suggest reading the books only, because you don't want your ideas to blend in with their books. Everyone has their own ideas, and sometimes you will come across a book that is fairly similar to yours. But, there should never be a book that is exactly like yours, from location, characters, and plots. If this happens to you, look into anyone whom you've shared information about your story to. This is why getting your original work copy written for $35 is a choice that should not be optional for a self-published author. I'll get into some of this information later, but non-disclosure forms are going to be a topic we discuss in this book as well for your beta readers. You want to create a team of trustworthy people that will not only help your growth but grow with you.

I want to touch on one last thing about creating original content. My hopes for you is that you be yourself. Be open, honest, and transparent in your work. Once you hit submit to send your book into the universe, it's like a weight is lifted. You may start small, but you have the potential to become big. Have the confidence of one hundred men or women that have your back. Find someone who you can celebrate all your small wins with. Building your team is a part of being original; they will all be unique and bring something different to the table.

You, my friend, will be in your own lane, and while you're busy creating, there will be people that don't understand why you're so passionate about writing. They don't understand why you love it so much. It's okay. I understand. I know exactly why you picked this book, and you started reading. I know that this won't be the only book you purchase or pick up that's about self-publishing. That's fine by me. I want this to be the best book that you pick up about self-publishing. I want this book to bring you so much joy, tools, and tips that you forever use it as a reference, or just for some inspiration. You now have all the tools to start creating something absolutely original.

// Chapter 3: Outline and Characters

Character:
A person used to describe a part in a story or movie.

Creating a story or informational book will change your life. It will change the way you think and the way you have conversations with other people. I highly recommend that you write all of your ideas down, whether they are in order or not. This will make the outlining process easier. Starting with a blank canvas can be pretty intimidating to a new author. In this chapter, I will give you detailed advice that could become a staple during your writing career.

/ Characters

If you already have your ideas or your character in mind, you will already have some traits written down about your character. During this process, when developing a character, I suggest you research characteristic traits, physical features, and get in full-mode. You need to become that character so that the emotions or the story you are telling becomes transparent.

I understand that when you are writing a self-help book that not all of this information will pertain to you. You still need to create an outline, and in your self-help book, you will be the character. Most of the advice will be coming from your perspective, so you can create a character outline for yourself to make sure you are giving as much of yourself to the reader.

Character Profile List

- Name
- Age
- General Physical Description
- Hometown
- Neighborhood (Suburban/Urban)
- Relationship Status
- Current Family

- Family Background (Parents, Marriage, Kids, etc.)
- Friends
- Other Close Relationships
- Relationship with Men/Women
- Job
- Style (Clothing)
- Religion
- Hobbies
- Sports
- Foods
- Strongest Personality Trait (Positive/Negative)
- Sense of Humor
- Pet Peeve
- Ambitions
- Philosophy of Life

You won't use all of these traits in your book, but it's always good to have them to look back on for your reference.
If your book has the potential to be a series, having this information and adding to it as each story grows, you will need it for a few years. Three pages of notes can turn into ten pages of detailed notes that will help you write a few books.

/ Outline

When the time comes to outline your book, this is where your story will unfold on sheets, a computer screen, or even in a journal. I have a few different ways that I outline. One is that I have a pocket journal that has scaled-down character profiles, with key points I can look back on without pulling out my sheets. I use this for when I'm writing on the go or when I just have my phone, but an idea needs to be jotted down.

Outlining your story can help you tell a story in just a few sheets. I like to hit major key points and then build the story while I'm writing. It's like filling in holes. I love when I can have a word or just a short sentence, and it sparked a 1500-word section in my story.

I want to be able to include some very important plots and information that your outline should include.

Plot List/Outline

- Working Title
- Genre
- Tense/POV
- Setting
- Incident
- Conflict

- Backstory
- Call to Action
- Obstacles
- Turning Point
- Climax
- Resolution
- Character Growth

These are just a few stages that you should be going through while you're writing.

One Incident could be the start of the story, and as you go on, it can become an internal or external conflict of what the characters want but can't have.

Give this character a problem. Once you have a problem, you need to create obstacles that will stop the character from reaching that next phase.

Characters should have a roller coaster ride of emotions. You want to give your readers a journey. With every problem, you will have to have a resolution. It could be a good end result or a bad one, depending on your genre and what type of story you are trying to write.

I want to switch gears really quick to give a positive note to my self-help book writers. You can have all of these same aspects in your book.

Whatever you are trying to help a reader with will have obstacles, problems, and resolutions. Like I said earlier, the main character in your story will be you, because everything you are telling them is from experience or a niche that you are an expert in.

That time when...

I read a book over the summer that brought me to tears (The Christ Family). I don't know the author personally, and I don't know her story. I do know that a lot of her material stems from past relationships or things that have happened in her life. Halfway through this story, I was very intrigued by the characters. I got to witness mysterious ways of one character, a naïve character, and a very strong character. There was a very intense scene in this book that I felt like we had switched places. I was now standing in that character's shoes—because at one point in my life I was that character. It was overwhelming, and by the time I tried to finish that section in the book, I was in tears. You want to be able to tell a story so good that the same type of emotion comes from your reader. As an author, some stories get deep, and that's why details in your outline and when you're narrating your story is so important. I messaged that author on Facebook to let her know that scene in her story really touched me. She had expressed her gratitude that I reached out to her as a fellow author.

This is the type of emotion you want to pull from a reader, whether it's a fiction or non-fiction book. Just by telling you my stories about how I have failed attempts at certain things will help you to understand why I chose to write this book. I know that not everyone has money just lying around ready to be invested in their dreams. Some of us still have to work a regular 9-5 and help others build their companies. It's the passion that will get you started in this industry, and it will be the readers you touch to keep you going.

I've given you some time to figure out character development and learn how to start from scratch. Now, I want to tell you some awesome tips to create characters that will keep your readers coming back.

1. Know your character
2. Your character should evolve
3. Your character's journey
4. Call to action
5. Study

Knowing your character is when your character profile sheet needs to be accessible. I like to keep a hard copy and a digital copy. Email it to yourself so that it can be found at a moment's notice. Once you write a book, people will constantly ask you about this book. You need to know your characters backward and forward.

The characters in your book should evolve. No character should not change. Once the character has a problem, he or she should learn from that mistake. If you're writing a series, your character should evolve. There should be a moment somewhere when something changes in his or her actions. The evolution of your characters' journey shouldn't be a fast one. Let's say, in the very first book of your series, your character drunk a glass of wine for the very first time; by the third book she now owns wine glasses and has a favorite wine. That could easily become her signature drink as the story progresses.

You must integrate your character with actions. People want to know how they will react in certain situations. It's easy when you choose the route that will bring emotions out of your readers. When you cause your readers to dislike a character, it makes your story appealing to other readers when they read the reviews.

I suggest you watch TV and read books that have a series. Study every day these series that people are intrigued by. Watch how the writers of shows develop these characters that possess certain traits. The shows that keep you coming back every week to see what happens next are a good example.

I can typically write a book with no outline. You may be able to do the same. I wouldn't recommend it with your first couple of books. The next set of tips I will give you will help you outline like a pro.

- Trust the process
- Be you

Once you decide to trust that this process will be easy, you will be successful.

Be comfortable in what you are bringing to the table. Your confidence will shine through your words.

Here is another surefire way to get the most out of your outlining experience:

- Send your character into a problem right away. You need a hook and bait tactic.
- Every time your characters try to solve the problem, give them a setback.
- Your character will appear to be helpless.
- Finally, your character's lessons will teach them how to solve his or her problem effortlessly.

These are all ways to go into writing and creating a flawless story. I love the idea of being able to tell a story from different points of views.

My favorite point of view is narrative; you can be very detailed and you paint a picture to your reader. You want them to feel like they are there for the story. I love reading a story to the point where it feels like I can smell the pumpkin spice in the air that the author mentions.

Writing from the first person and third person point of view are also two great point of views that a lot of authors write from as well.

Two main genres are Fiction & Non-Fiction

/ Fiction

The fiction world is a huge pot of interesting stories, ideas for the creative mind. I love writing fiction stories because I get to create something different. You get to push the envelope when it comes to how far you push your characters. You can make a thriller story turn crime or romance. That's what I love about fiction; I feel that there are no rules because it's like going into a creative fantasy. You want to do one main thing: draw the reader in.

/ Non-fiction

Non-fiction writing can be about you or someone you know. It can range from all sorts of topics and sometimes not even people. As an author, you can make a living off of ghostwriting a non-fiction story about someone else. If I had a penny for every time someone said their life is a book...

Get out there and help an aspiring storyteller write her life story. You can create a contract that will allow your name to be printed and have a set amount of royalties or lifetime royalties. This is called creating another income stream.

/ Synopsis (an outline of the plot of a book)

A synopsis gives readers a general idea of what your book is about without completely telling the story. This doesn't need a full chapter by itself, but it is a very important part of your outline. You can either write your synopsis first, or you can write it last. It just depends on what is most comfortable for you.

Your synopsis will be your brief summary every time you talk about your book. I want to provide you with some key points that you will need in your synopsis:

- A Narrative
- Action Voice
- Dynamic Point of View
- Story Development
- Clarity

The narrative will include an explanation of the plot or the problem. You will need to provide clues as to how the story will end or may end. Summarize the story's development. Make sure the voice in your synopsis is strong and use the third person. Remember to be clear and that less is more. You need to make sure your story is unique, and it sets you apart from other stories. Synopsis are generally one to two pages long. Because you are also your own publisher, you will basically be the creator/creative director of your own success.

When giving tips, it's also my duty to give you some do not tips:

- Mentioning too many characters or events
- Including too many details and plot twist
- Unnecessary descriptions
- Make sure you wrote a full synopsis, not a back cover summary

When you self-publish, there are a lot of things you have to learn. This is why I'm giving so much detailed information here. I want you to be able to use this book as your holy grail during your self-publishing process. It's easy to give you tips with a few bullets in less than 3000 words, but having this book to come back to time and time again to help you through each step of the process makes this a lifetime investment.

/ Book Blurb

A book blurb differs from a synopsis; so does a media kit. I will probably talk about that later on in the book. Your book blurb is the back cover of your book; it's like a sales pitch. It pulls the reader in after she picks up your book.
Here are the items that should be featured on your book blurb:

- A touch of plot
- Words that resonate with the images
- Main characters named and identified
- Idea of setting
- A question or hint or mystery
- Controversy
- Quotes from the book or previous book
- Length
- About the author

When you provide a touch of your plot, it should be the most amazing first sentence that will sum up your entire book. When you use eye-catching words to create an image, it will draw your readers in mid-sentence. Knowing the character's name and his or her title or job description also allows the reader to find books that may resonate with them. Including a key location and pose a question will bring about questions to the reader. They will want to find the answer by opening the pages of your book. When you write controversially and use hyperbole to make your book stand out along with quotes from reviews, you have higher chances of having a breakout story. Your blurb should be about 100-150 words, and this does not include your About the Author.

You're About the Author can include your picture on the back, along with an amusing and subtle three to four sentence bio about you.

I love to include stories to show you that even after you read all of this and follow each step, you'll possibly still make a mistake.

I cannot stress the fact that you are your own publisher; you can go back and make changes to your book at any time. Whether it's the words or the cover, you can change it. How I outlined my very first book:

I had this bright idea to take the plunge from writing poetry into writing a book. I thought to myself, how hard could this be? I see millions of books everywhere, these people had to start from somewhere too, right? Well, I figured I should actually write the book first and then everything else would fall into place.

My first outline was born. On some 8x10 computer paper sitting at my Walmart desk with my desktop Compaq computer. I had an idea to write a story about my ex-boyfriends. I don't have many, but I wanted to write about love.

The title Journeys of the Heart was born. I just didn't write about my ex-boyfriends. I created six dynamic young ladies who all had promising careers. The challenge for them came when it was time to find love, fall in love, and stay in love. My first book. I was excited.

It sat at a standstill for about a year. I forgot about it, and then I moved to another state. I found my pages of Journeys of the Heart inside a plastic sleeve. My excitement was renewed, and I put the finishing touches on the book. Along with that came lots of research. It paid off, because I found this amazing website that I could self-publish my book for free. My very first book was self-edited, a bad choice that I learned from, and then I used the website's free cover service. At the time I wasn't familiar with cover sizes and other aspects. The moral of the story is, you can start for free, but once you start, you will want to spend money on your dream. I want to show you how to make the most out of self-publishing without breaking the bank. The hard work and long hours will turn into residual income for the rest of your life.

The best thing you can do is outline your book with as many details as possible. Sometimes we need one or two endings, or the characters end up being harder to identify with, and you want to start over. Sometimes you will delete an entire chapter that you spent hours on writing because now it doesn't fit with the story.

Creating your vision from scratch is rewarding. You can craft an entire story with your hands, and once you read it, you will be able to find your passion again every single time.
The outline is only the beginning, but it is also very vital to your finished product.

I don't want you to be stressed out about writing an award-winning book. I want you to be happy about writing a book that shows it can compete with the best. I want it to be a standout project.

I will go over a few more reasons why you should write and outline just in case you feel that you can make it without writing one.

You will probably have fewer chances of having writer's block because you have already outlined your story, and you know the flow of how it will move. It will reduce having to do rewrites and fewer turnarounds from an editor. You will be able to iron out any problems with the storyline before you get started with the first draft. It gives you more room to be creative. Your character will have strong characteristics, and the goals of the story will show more clarity. When you have a strong character that you will be able to outline every detail with, you will be able to create many dimensions of that character.

Bottom line, don't ever start your story without an outline, and create breathtaking characters that will create controversy.

/ Narrative

In the next few pages, I want you to take some of these bullet points and create your very first character. This will be your main character. I want you to take some of his backstories and throw him into the first problem that he will face in your novel. Next, I want you to be able to outline the first few chapters of your book until you get the hang of it.
This will help you create your own character and outline sheets that will fit your story or your genre of writing.

// Chapter 4: Book Cover and Title

The first thing you will see is a Book Cover of a prospective book that you would want to read. Whether you are browsing in a bookstore, or online looking for a new read. We often look for things that are attractive to our eye. Breathtaking images that tell a story without opening a page or reading the synopsis. Book covers and titles go hand and hand.

Ex. My first book mistake

My book's title is Journeys of the heart. I choose this title because It was about friends going through different relationship stages.

My first cover was pink, and it had a cute little cupcake on the front. The cupcake had nothing to do with the story.

I was just excited to self-publish my first book. I later learned that when my audience started to get larger. Most people turned away from my book cover.

Now today I can admit it was cute, but it was a very amateur mistake.

This process should be started early on once you decide the direction of your book. You should never rush someone to finish your book cover. Once you decide where you will start looking for a designer. You will need to have a plan.

Here is a list of places and suggestions that will help you find someone to create a cover for you within your $100 budget.

/ Graphic Designers

Fiverr – I'm spent about $5 for an eBook cover and $20 for a full paperback cover. Most of the time they include a 3D image and the source file. One of my favorite book designers on Fiverr is Jeshart.

Facebook – Everyone is starting a business online. I suggest you do a quick Facebook shout out for any new graphic designers who are looking to build their portfolios. They will offer less expensive work and also be very eager for your business. In return, they will work with you to create just what you want.

Local College/Friends – I would reach out to your local colleges that have different design programs to see if there are any college students that you can help build their portfolios. This could be a win/win for you.

I recommend for a first book not spending more than $30 on a complete cover.

You should also have a plan surrounding your book cover. You need to have at least 3-5 ideas of what you want it to look like. You can sketch it or even write down key points of items that you want your cover to have. You never want to leave the fate of your book cover in someone else's hands. Your cover should tell a story or at least raise questions about what the book is about. You want the reader to be curious enough to approach your book.

I like to envision the obstacles in my story and the main character to come up with an idea of an image that would be perfect for the story.

My second book, New Birth & New Life, was surrounded around a wedding and a new baby. This has to be my most flawless cover ever. It shows half of the brides face in a beautiful wedding gown. The colors blend well, and the words don't fade to the back because the picture is flawless I get lots of questions about the story. Every time I look this cover, I'm in awe.

Because you are choosing to self-publish you have to go above and beyond to make your book stand out. Here are a few steps to help you create an amazing book cover.

1. Create a mood board
2. Research another cover with similar genres
3. Sketch or write down what you want
4. Know your resolution/pixels requirement

Create a mood board that has images, a color palette, words or objects that will create the ideas you have for your potential book cover.

I love looking at well-known author's covers for inspiration. I look at them as vets in this industry, and their tactics are tried and true.

The sketching part is fun for me because whatever vision I have I can create it on a piece of paper. No matter how good of an artist I maybe. It gives my graphic designer something to work with.

Knowing what pixels or resolution your cover needs to be in is very important. We will talk about the different type of publishing channels later on in the book. But, depending on what type of self-publishing company you go with this will be important. You will need to give your graphic designer these requirements so that your upload process for your book will be smooth.

The main things your book cover should include are the front cover with your title, sub-title, and your name. If you are a national best-selling author, you can choose to include that on your cover as well. Some people like to include a quick but short review of their book, possibly from a beta reader, which we will also talk about later in this book. On your back cover, include your book blurb along with your short bio. I highly recommend adding a professional headshot of yourself on the back of your book. If you would like to remain anonymous, then this is a step you can skip. Your ISBN numbers will automatically be included by your print-on-demand company when it goes to print at the bottom right corner of your book on the back cover.

My best advice to you when picking a graphic designer is to be completely involved; pick a designer who will either have unlimited revisions or a minimum of three revisions. Never be afraid to tell your graphic designer you do not like something. After all, it's your money and your book. If you feel your graphic designer has not delivered to your expectations, it's okay to use one of those backups ideas and go back to the drawing board. I remember I was not satisfied with a cover that my designer kept sending me. It wasn't giving me a "wow" reaction. So, I told him I wanted to change the concept, and we came up with something beautiful. This is why we plan for things to go wrong, even though it sounds negative. If you're prepared, you can just reroute your plan and still come out with an amazing product.

Title:

the name given to something (such as a book, song, or movie) to identify or describe it.

I think coming up with a title is the fun part when it comes to writing your book. I have an eight-book series, and I have come up with every single name for my books based on the characters and the obstacles that they were faced with. I love the creative part of coming up with a name that will be in the homes of many people. To others, it may seem easy to name a book, but each story becomes more and more meaningful to you.

A few things that I do when coming up with titles:

1. Copyright Search
2. Amazon Search
3. Patent/Trademark Search
4. Library Catalog Search
5. Franchise Bookstore Search

These five steps can help you to not duplicate another author's title. I've seen it a few times, and it really is sometimes an honest mistake.

Right now, Amazon is the place to go to purchase just about anything, and with Amazon Prime, you can have free two-day shipping. So it's only right that one of the places your book will be searched for first is on Amazon. I love that when I name my book, either none show up in the e-books or print books section. I know that means when interested readers type in my book's name, it should be the first book to show up for that name search. This puts me at the top of the page, and no one has to search down the list for my book.

I would also do legal checks that include checking for the patent and trademark names at www.copyright.gov. You should also get familiar with this site to have your own books copyrighted. It's always good to check online franchise bookstores titles. A big one is Barnes & Noble. I would also visit my local library and check out their titles. You can never be too sure.

Let's talk about what makes a great title. Sometimes it's a simple process, and then other times, it's a long process to find the right title:

- Use Descriptive Titles
- Simple Language

Using descriptive titles will answer certain questions. You have to have some type of mystery in the title. I want you to think about the acronym WIIFM (What's In It For Me?). When readers pick this book up, they want to know the answer to that question. So your book has to have something descriptive. Also use simple language. Don't use words that only a few people will know, no matter what type of book you are writing. If things ever go left, and your books aren't selling with the current title, never be afraid to change the title.

Your title's length doesn't matter, either. You can have a long or short title, but always stick with those two important factors that make great titles.

The road to success is not easy, and it's always cool to throw hints out there. Sometimes we get these really great ideas in our heads. We become stuck on an idea. But then you're the only one who is ecstatic about it. Your audience loses interest and the momentum dies down. I like the idea of keeping people guessing.

I found out that the website www.lulu.com has this unique title tool; it will help you determine what percentage your title will sell. I've never used it, but I feel that if you want to get a feel for what you are looking at, you should give it a try. Here are some things you should also do to see if your title will live up to the hype:

I love being able to look at what successful authors that I admire are doing. I want to study their ways and test things out that are working for them. It's possible that maybe one idea will work for me. I know some of the types sound redundant, but there are many ways to do a different task:

You should study other successful books in your genre, like the ones that have been best-sellers for more than a month or so. You need to learn how those titles are being effective and who they are reaching. How many reviews does the book have? The fonts, and design—these are all things you should pay attention to.

Think about the different themes of your book. This should help you come up with title ideas. I'm going to go back to elementary school right now. Remember when you read a book and needed to write down the main idea, the setting, and a few details? This step can also help with your book cover.

- You should familiarize yourself with different popular titles. Look at the New York Times best seller list. Learn their structures and what they have in common. When you find the common factor, you will be able to put this towards your new titles.

- Having numerous amount of sources and feedback will put you at the top of your game. That's right, our author game. That was supposed to be a joke. Get it?
I hoped you at least chuckled.

We've talked about outlines, characters, book covers, and titles. So you should be in the stages of everything falling into place, and now you need to get to the technical stuff. Right now, I just wanted you to get comfortable with writing a book. It's easy for me to say to stop at this chapter right now if you don't have a book outline written. I don't want you to put this book down, but I want you to work through it at your own pace.

I love building anticipation for anything, so it's only right that when the time comes for you to reveal your title and cover, it should be a big production. I love giving sneak peeks of different things, whether it's excerpts from the upcoming book or baiting my audience online.

I love these catch phrases:

"If I get x amount of likes I'll reveal my new title."

"I will be releasing the new book cover at (insert time)."

"Today I'm giving a sneak peek of a chapter from my new book."

These are things that will provide curiosity.

While we are on the topic, I want to provide some suggestions on how to brand your book once you decide on the title and cover.

Having a 3D cover that's transparent and ready for marketing your book will be coming up soon in this book. I want you to think months in advance when you are getting ready to release your book.

Getting a domain name with your book title and an author email address will also help your book stand out. The site should be all about your book. When we talk about beta readers in the next chapter, you will be able to include reviews on this site. Your bio and book blurb will all be a good fit for this site. It'll provide informational items to keep everyone in the loop of what's going on with your book promotion.

I love the whole idea of creating something from scratch. At first, it doesn't have anything; it's like a plain sheet of blank computer paper.

Then you come in with your fancy ideas and your creative mind. Next thing you know, you're writing the end and you have designed a book from cover to cover. There is no greater feeling than completing that project.

Worksheet

In the next couple of pages, you will be able to write down a few different titles and do a cross elimination of which ones have been used, and based on all the tips I've given you, which one will sell the best.

There will also be an area for you to sketch your book cover You can paste or draw pictures and include different color schemes to see which will work best for your book cover.

Titles

- ☐ ....
- ☐ ....
- ☐ ....
- ☐ ....
- ☐ ....
- ☐ ....
- ☐ ....
- ☐ ....
- ☐ ....
- ☐ ....
- ☐ ....
- ☐ ....

// Chapter 5: Editor and Beta Readers

Editor:

someone who edits and revises written material.

We are getting to the part of the book that holds the meat and potatoes—the parts where you start to see where you will spend money. If you ever want to be taken seriously in this industry, you'll need an editor. I'm not talking about your mom or your friend who likes to correct your text messages. I'm referring to someone who is dedicated to creating good content. Someone who knows what to look for in a book. Someone who can provide you with valuable information and help you with the direction of your book. It's okay to have your friend look at it and make suggestions if you both have different perspectives. Just please, hire an editor to look it over once, twice, or three times to ensure you are putting out quality work.

Once you finish your manuscript and type the end and you get to see all those pages on your computer, it can be very overwhelming. I suggest you print it out to get a good look at it. Make notes and suggestions on the sides and go back in and make those changes. This would be considered your rough draft. After making those necessary changes, I would then send it to your editor. Whoever you decide on, make sure you establish a good working relationship with them. Let them know what you are looking for, and even your weaknesses, so that they can pay even more attention to those issues. When negotiating a price, it usually goes by word count. My novellas are usually around 20,000 words. I've paid around $30 on editing, and I am also subscribed to this monthly service called Grammarly that helps me with some of the technical stuff I miss. I would make sure your editor can provide you with at least two to three rounds of edits.

The biggest thing in choosing your editor is to have communication and understanding.

I will probably recommend Fiverr a few more times in this book, but it's because it's a great service with some really talented people. The prices range from $5-100+ dollars, but it's well worth it. Another service where you can find lots of freelance editors is at Upwork (www.upwork.com). This site allows you to post jobs and search for freelancers to provide a service for you. It's a very easy process to set up. I love that about both sites. They're easy to navigate and the platforms have amazing reviews.

Here are a few things that you should look for when searching for an editor:

- Look for someone with experience
- Positive energy and work ethic
- Look in the right places
- Interview their past clients
- Interview the editor and have her work on a sample chapter

As you can tell, this won't be an easy process. Looking for an editor can happen when you are half-way through your book to make sure you have time to find the right editor when you're done.

When you first start looking, it's always good to look for referrals by asking friends. Some people come highly recommended. Once you find a few people—I say five is a good number of candidates to start with—you should ask for their resume, including titles and publications they have worked on. This is basically inquiring about their work. You want to be able to have a good working relationship with whoever you choose. I love scheduling meetings to either talk to someone over the phone or via a video chat. That way you can see if you are having good chemistry. You don't want to work with anyone who makes you cringe, or who makes you regret the decision to work with him. When you start a conversation, most of the time you tell right away whether or not it's a good fit The Internet is filled with lots of variety. Feel free to choose a platform that is right for you to choose an editor. Once you have a list of the editor's publications and/or resume, let them know that you may be reaching out to some of their clients. I suggest you have a simple template for inquiring about prior service; you can use it for future service inquiries as well, whether looking for a graphic designer or some PR work. Getting feedback from prior clients is good, but doing your own interviewing will make things run even smoother. I would come up with a list of questions that you would like to ask your potential editor, and asking her if she would mind working on a sample chapter with you so you can see how well you two work together. If you have to pay a consultation fee, negotiate that price be taken off of the full price if you decide to use that Editor. Everything is negotiable. EVERYTHING. Never feel like you are selling yourself short or that you can't talk about coming up with a plan.

Goodreads (www.goodreads.com) is a site that you sign up for as well. It's good for authors and readers to learn more information about certain books. I came across this group called Editio Self-Publishing. People post editors they like; Goodreads is also a good place to find resources.

I want to cover two more things when you are in the process of editing your book:

Proofreading:

reading (printer's proofs or other written or printed material) and marking any errors.

Your editor is amazing, I know, but these two steps are completely optional. I wouldn't feel right if I didn't make sure you knew about every single tool that could help your book. Having someone who can proofread your book even after your editor went through all three hundred pages of your manuscript can provide the changes your book needs to provide a better reading experience for your readers. A proofreader will make sure to catch any errors that may have been overlooked by the editor. You can find free services for proofreading, or you can use two separate pairs of eyes to help you look over your story. Whatever you decide, make sure you make this decision in the best interest of your budget.

A few sites that I would like to recommend:

- Grammarly (www.grammarly.com)
- SlickWrite (www.slickwrite.com)
- ProofreadBot (www.proofreadbot.com)

Some services are free, and some require a fee. Again, always use your best judgment if you are trying to stick to your budget.

Copyediting:
editing text by checking its consistency and accuracy.

A copyeditor checks for accuracy throughout your book, making sure the words you are using are consistent with their meanings. A copyeditor can provide change to make sure the style of your writing flows continuously as the pages go on, and formatting your pages to make sure it's right for your book.

You can look for copyeditors at these sites:

- Upwork (www.upwork.com)
- Fiverr (www.fiverr.com)
- Freelancer (www.freelancer.com)

I've told you all of this to tell you: your editor should provide all of this. That's if you find an editor who knows that all of these services can be bundled into a package. Even though you have these outlets to other services, finding that one editor who can do all three will make your life so much easier.

Let's fast forward to that moment when you receive your final, edited copy from your editor. You look at it in amazement. Thinking to yourself, I did it! I finally put the fears behind me, and I wrote a book! I can see the excitement in your eyes.

I'll be the first to say, I'm proud of you!
Now that you've approved all changes and you've stared at that final copy for a few days, it's time to move on to the next step. Finding someone to read and give you feedback on it before you publish it.

It's okay to have it up and ready for preorder; you're gearing up to start your marketing plan. But now you need some trusted sources that will be your eyes and ears about your book. That's right—you need a beta reader, or beta readers, depending on what your needs are.

Beta Reader: Someone who critiques your work, and provides a thorough review. Beta Readers can provide a list of errors or information that you request when choosing Beta Readers for your new book. Some Beta Readers also leave first release day reviews along with recommending your work to others.

Gifting books on release day in hopes that the lucky people who receive it leave reviews within the first week is like waiting for paint to dry on the wall. I can't tell you how many people I've gifted a book to, and I'm still waiting on reviews from a year ago. I don't know if they read it or not. Maybe they didn't like it. It could have been that they just weren't my target audience.

A way to ensure this doesn't happen and that you have at least two five-star reviews on release day (that would totally put you on the map) is to look into having a few beta readers on your time. The rule is that they usually work for free books, and a signed paperback would be awesome for someone who takes time out to provide crucial feedback for your book. Here are some tips for working with beta readers:

- Don't give them an unfinished book
- Ask them about the format
- Provide structure
- Don't take it personal
- Return the favor

Most of the times you want feedback or a review on your final work. It's imperative that you give your beta reader a finished book. In your eyes, it's perfect, so now you need to hand it off to someone who doesn't know you, but who also has experience with providing helpful tips. You want the honest review on what you are putting out. When you get ready to send a finished book, make sure you provide the beta reader with the format that they are most comfortable with. This is when having your book under copyright comes in handy. I like to send in Mobi format; Kindle has a free app anyone can download, and it provides a seamless reading experience. Your reader may choose to have it sent in .pdf, or even Microsoft Word. They may want it printed out. All of these ways will be protected because your work is protected. I'll talk about having them sign a non-disclosure agreement a little later. Providing a checklist of things you are looking for in your story will help this process run smoothly. If you don't provide the structure, you can't be picky about what kind of critique you get back. When you get the notes back from your beta reader, remember that they are helping you make your book better. Never take it personally; you needed this information to make sure you are putting out quality work. If you enjoyed working with a certain reader and they express working with you again in the future, I would go ahead and put them in as a permanent reader. Rewarding your reader with a signed print book if it's available will also keep them happy. They are probably more likely to organically share your book with others without it sounding like a sales pitch. Now that you know what a Beta Reader is and what they do to help you in the process of self-publishing your book, I'll help you find beta readers to join your team.

The total cost for this service should be $0.

Where to find beta readers:

- Social Media
- Referrals
- Goodreads
- Local Writing Groups
- My Writers Circle (www.mywriterscircle.com)
- Writing.com

These are just a few idea of places where beta readers hang out. I found a recent beta readers just by sending out a quick tweet. We exchanged emails a few times, and she is now on board for my next book. When searching, you also need to make sure they fit your target audience, or they can be of assistance to you.

Here are some things you need to look for in your future beta reader:

- read your genre
- understand your guidelines
- likes to read
- not afraid to critique
- trustworthy
- communicative

It's only right to have standards and rules when it comes to your work. So let's talk about the technical stuff.

I would rather have some type of paperwork to protect me and my beta reader. Make sure you have a non-disclosure agreement about reproducing the story or a similar story that is under copyright; it will result in a lawsuit. To make sure your beta reader is given some sort of relief, you should provide in writing what they will receive in return for their review on Release Day. I would normally provide a print copy of the book signed by me. I would also go ahead and provide them with the next job of the next book to secure a spot as a beta reader. The goal is to keep everyone happy. If you default on your promise, your beta reader has the right to seek counsel. Sometimes we don't like to talk about the failures or the what ifs if something goes wrong, but in this case, I need to prepare you, and we should stay ahead of the game with problem solving.

Now that was a good bit of information, and I feel like I'm leading you in a great direction. You will be more than ready to tackle your self-published book.

You want to know a funny, but a truly profitable story? My first book—you know, the ultimate fail, self-published first book.

Yeah that one. It had so much potential to be my first best-seller, but the knowledge I had was lacking. I wasn't afraid to admit that I had no clue what I was doing. I just knew I wrote a book and I wanted it to be on CreateSpace. You'll learn about them in the next few chapters. I wanted an actual book that I could put in my hands. I love to read, and a few of my favorite authors are Kimberla Roby Lawson and Keith Lee Johnson. I have many of their paperback books, and now I was about to have my own. So, I followed the easy steps to set my book up. I didn't know if it looked right or not. I tried my best to edit. (Spellcheck.) Horrible idea. Everything was ready. Do you know that I skipped two major steps that I just mentioned in this book? I had NO Editor and NO beta readers. What was I thinking? The weird thing is that this book is currently the most-sold book I have. Insert shock face. Yeah, your personality and character can sell a horrible book.

The sad part about it is that no one told me it was horrible. They all loved it. I have good reviews from the books, and I even now have loyal readers who enjoy anything I write. Do you have the chin rub emoji in mind for that last sentence? Yeah, I couldn't figure it out either. Why was no one telling me how horribly it was edited, and that the format looked crazy? I realized this on my own a year later when I decided to change the cover first, and then I had an editor to look at my first three chapters.

The feedback was amazing. He provided me with such in-depth feedback, it made me realize that I could have gone deeper with the story in return. I felt like I might have shortchanged my readers. Again, no one told me. Well, I'm telling you. Strive for quality and not quantity.

There are lots of people who can write a book in a month and put it out. I have seen it so many times. Once it's released, they have to apologize for careless mistakes. Don't let that be you. Your readers will understand if it takes longer for you to put out another book.

I know we all feel the pressure being a writer or content creator. Being organized will most definitely help you when it comes to putting your book together. The book will continue to teach you valuable information as we move along. Most of your foundation is already laid.

I want to leave you with a few reminders:

Don't get stressed out. Slow down and breathe.
You are creating a masterpiece.
Quality last longer than quantity.
You're going be an awesome author.
Use every tool in this book.

Here are a few affirmations that will help you when you get stuck:

- I am like a Dr. Seuss without green eggs and ham
- My goal is simple. Hit publish!
- When in doubt, shout it OUT!

I hope that I am providing not only some inspiration but some serious comedic relief. I have to laugh—it's just my personality to be fun. Your readers will soon get to know your personality. If you're sarcastic, then that's a trait they will remember, and make sure you add some of that in your book.

As we start embarking on your marketing plan and formatting your book (which are also very important, essential things to help you wrap things up), I hope you were able to grasp the importance of hiring an editor who can provide you with more than one service. The goal here is to find someone who is good and who is good for your book. Don't forget that everything is negotiable. Always stay on track with your budget, and never skip out on the pre-planning. Plan for everything. Remember, even plan for problems. Map out those possible solutions. I hope that during this process you will find a great editor and a team of amazing beta readers.

Happy Editing!

Worksheet

My Top 3 Editors

Name: ....

Website: ....

Contact Information: ....

....

....

Rate: ....

Name: ....

Website: ....

Contact Information: ....

....

....

....

Rate: ....

Name: ....

Website: ....

Contact Information: ....

....

....

....

Rate: ....

// Chapter 6: Marketing Plan

Marketing:
a way to get out information about products and service you are offering. You market to your target audience to drive sales for your book or business.

It's never too early to start your marketing plan. You'll not only need a plan, but you'll need tools. I'm here to help you create a plan that will help you gain anticipation for your new book and create a group of readers that will be ready for every release here on out. I can tell you one thing. Marketing is a lot of work, but there are lots of tools out there that can help you start in advance and to keep the momentum up. So, let's jump right into it.

I want to say that once you are half-way through your book, you should give a tease. Whether it's your mock-up book cover or sneak peeks into your book, people love when you're giving something away. Once you decide on your book title, you should go ahead and grab that domain name. Once you have a book cover, you should go ahead and use that to create marketing tools. I'll go in-depth on what type of tools or things you should offer.

/ Marketing Plan

- Book Domain Name
- Landing Page
- Give Away Something (bookmarks, downloads, worksheets)
- Social Media
- Interviews
- Face to Face
- Library
- Scheduling Content
- Hiring PR (This could be by using a service or someone part-time)
- Book Blog Tours
- Marketing Tools
- Bookmarks
- Business cards
- T-shirts
- YouTube Videos
- Banners

When starting out on this journey, grabbing your domain
name for your book is a pretty good idea. If you have a series,
or if you feel you'll write more books, you can just grab the
domain name for yourself as an Author. I decided to go the
route of using my name because I have different genres and
also enjoy blogging. I used www.wordpress.org to set up
my site. If you're not ready for all the fancy plugins, www.
Blogger.com is still a very good platform. My old blog is
still up and running, having awesome views on the Blogger
platform. A landing page can be used for a few different
things: if you want people to sign up for an event or a course
you're offering, or if you are trying to collect emails for
email marketing. This is where you will offer that free item.
People love to know what they are giving you their email
for. I suggest if you start a newsletter, be sure to stay on a
schedule. If you say you're going to send out a newsletter
weekly, make sure your readers know it's coming weekly on
that day. If you won't have one that week, let them know. The
worst thing you can do is have your readers waiting.

I know that sometimes social media is hard to stay on top of.
Things are forever changing, but it's also exciting. Staying
up to date by reading TechCrunch and other technology
blogs will help you learn what's changing and how you can
use it for your book marketing. I suggest that you create a
Facebook Fan Page, Instagram, and Twitter to stay in touch
with your readers.

If your wanting to reach new audiences and get the word out, you should reach out to bloggers who are dedicated to doing book reviews and telling their readers about new books. Try your hand at radio interviews; it's another way to get the word out. I've started the radio journey myself. I'm so shocked at the amount of authors who also have radio shows or podcasts.

This suggestion is my favorite: getting out in your community and talking to people. I love that you can print out whatever you want on some card stock or cut up sheets of paper and walk around downtown and had out your information to strangers. I guarantee you will find readers, and a few of them will actually visit your site because they are curious.

Moving along to the best resource out there: the library! Visit your local libraries and find out what kind of workshops they have and if they have anything special they offer to local authors. This can be a major way to connect with readers. Most libraries accept donations of your book to put on their shelf. Talking to them about a book signing would be awesome for your sales and visibility.

If you need a way to stay on top of your social media content, you should try out some services like Co Schedule, Buffer, and Hootsuite. These can help you schedule your content for as long and far out as you need to. A lot of the services can send out your content to numerous social media accounts as well. I absolutely love this part of marketing. The services help you see what posts are effective and how many people they are reaching.

Hiring PR help can also be super useful to your marketing. Someone who knows how to get in touch with contacts will be very beneficial. You can use Fiverr, Upwork, or Fancy Hands (www.fancyhands.com) to find someone to hire temporarily.

Start reaching out to book bloggers or find an online community that caters to blog book tours. Have an inquiry email ready to send to the site owner to inquire about hosting a blog tour on their website. This can be an awesome tool for your book promotion. If you choose KDP Select, which you will learn about in the next few chapters, you can go on a five day blog tour when you schedule your book on a free promotion. Make a list of potential book bloggers you would like to work with. Then send each of them an email, give it about two weeks to get a response, and then move on to the next few.

Resources are easy to research, and some are more useful than others. Bookmarks can be a great tool, especially if it's the theme of your book and your information is printed on it. It could double as a business card. If you decide to be the one who packages and ships your books, sending a free bookmark with every purchase would be wonderful.

Business cards are an absolute must for any entrepreneur or author. You need them when you are networking and meeting new people. The more creative your business card is, the more you will be remembered. I love that when you start to create your brand colors and mood boards, you are crafting something amazing with your vision.

I've seen more and more authors using t-shirt marketing as a new strategy. Whether it's with the name of their reading groups or shows a stand-out character on the shirt, I love the idea of having shirts with my logo on them. This is an awesome idea to me.

Building an amazing YouTube channel that will become a new platform for you can help you reach another group or audience of people. My YouTube channel provides so much support from strangers. I would also look at different BookTube videos and reach out to these content creators who can help with book marketing for your new release. During your first book signing, you will need some essentials, like banners and table décor. You can choose how to decorate your table, but having a standing banner should be at the top of your list of marketing tools.

Comparative Titles (Comp Titles):
other works that are comparable to your own book

Having a list of comp titles can help people place your upcoming book in the right genre or know where you fit in with other authors. This will help your visibility when you are a new author. If you're a new author with maybe one book from self-publishing, this could help you when working on press releases. You can say, "Hey, you know that book Think and Grow Rich? It's a modern day version of that. You'll find my book just as useful."

Here are a few tips to help you choose the right comp titles:

- Choose titles that are in the same genre and category
- Be specific
- Don't make comp titles complicated
- Character comp
- Your favorite movie could be a comp title
- Never set the bar too high

When choosing comp titles, you need to think about the genre of your book. Then think about if there was a table for books just like yours, all with the same theme in a bookstore. What table would you be on? A table with superheroes, or a table with strong female leads? You need to make sure that your titles are clear. If your title could be placed on a few different tables, you need to make sure you break it down.

It's always good to look at new books to choose your comp titles from. Never feel like you have to use more than one book. That makes things complicated, especially if the books don't possess the same tones. This could easily confuse your future readers. I love this idea. When you're struggling to find a book that you can compare your book to, and you keep drawing a blank, look at your main character and see if he or she has any qualities that match a book you've recently read, or maybe even a title from your past that your main character reminds you of. Don't limit yourself to book titles. Movies and TV shows can be a source as well. I would bank on newer shows, like Queen Sugar, Shameless, or even How to Get Away with Murder. If you have a character who is as persistent and quick on her feet like Annalise, this would be a great chance to get people interested. I know I've gotten you all excited, but don't oversell your book with comp titles. If you set the bar high and your story doesn't deliver, be ready to bounce back and try again. You can't compare your story to Grease if it's more like The Little Rascals.

These tools will help you get your title ready for release date. It also helps when it's time to get into the "readers also read" category.

/ Creating your Marketing Plan

If my guide doesn't help you create your marketing plan, I'm going to create a list of things you need to create your own marketing plan that will fit your needs:

- Define your audience
- Where is your audience (online)
- Budget
- Guest Blog Post
- Inside Connections
- Reviews and Testimonials
- Email List
- Book Trailer
- Interviews
- Speaking Engagements
- Market Price
- Order Fulfillment
- Plan
- Execute

/ Define your audience

There are ways to define your audience if you already have books available for the public. Look at your Facebook, Amazon, and Goodreads accounts to see who are reading your books. If you don't have any books out yet, check out similar books to yours and see the range of ages or type of readers who read those books. If you have an email list, you can also gain some insight on your readers from that as well. Once you narrow down your audience, you can identify your groups:

- Stay-at-home mom blogger in South Carolina
- Twenty-five- to thirty-five-year-old content creators who vlog or blog
- Aspiring writers who don't have a large social following

This stage is vital to your bookselling. Once you find these people, you can start selling. Remember, if you are selling a children's book, you need to target the parents.

/ Where is your audience (online)

Browse leading blogs to find where your target readers hang out to get the news on the latest books. In this day and age, you have "bookstagrammers" and "BookTube." Find bookstagrammers by looking up that hashtag on Instagram and looking at the posts. Look for books that are similar to yours and check out those content creator profiles and like their content. Start a dialogue and network. BookTube, on

YouTube, is full of readers discussing books they read and are currently obsessed with. Most of these video content creators will have an email in their description bar. I say to reach out to them and let them read your work. This could be a really good marketing move for your paperbacks. You can easily access your target market through social media.

/ Budget

Depending on the amount of your budget, you can use ads or promotional websites or companies to assist in your book marketing. Facebook has teamed up with Instagram, and you can sponsor amazing content to reach your target audience on both platforms. They also show you who's liking your posts and where they are located. It's good to know that maybe your target market reaches older women or men as well. This data will help you when you know who you are writing for. Your budget can change at anytime, so make sure you move things around so that you can still get all the necessary things you need for your launch done. Making a list of what needs to be paid for by priority can knock out the can and can't dos.

/ Guest blog post

You should create at least five possible blog posts that you can use to be a guest blogger on sites. These posts should be straightforward, and you should be able to tell your readers about what your book will help them with and what problems it will solve. Readers love a list, and they love to learn something. No one wants to read anything that won't give them some type of help or solution. If you need to, talk to the blogger to ask him or her what type of stories or information his or her readers enjoy. Once you know a little more information about the blogger's audience, you can create something that works for you and still keep the audience happy.

/ Inside connections

Round up all your family and friends who have the inside connection to someone semi-famous. Get them to send you their contact information so that you can reach out to him or her to send a free book. If you are a part of lots of reading groups, I suggest you reach out to the authors or the readers who have a large following. Have your friends and family in on the fun by offering an incentive to see how many people they can refer to visit your site or your social media accounts. This way, it creates a competition for your family to enjoy your release.

/ Reviews and Testimonials

Make a list of people who you know that maybe will give a testimonial or a review about your work. It could even be your beta readers. If you have a quote from someone in your field, it will make things even better, especially if they are a popular author. I would say revisit your inside connection list as well for quotes. A strong five beta reader team can do wonders for you on release day.

/ Email List

The email list that I mentioned before will be a great help to get newsletters out to your subscribers. Having an email list can be a big part of your marketing on release day and the days leading up to that. Creating this list and keeping your readers updated about the progress by providing sneak peeks to them through email will also build the anticipation for your release. The landing page with information about your book will help to bring in new readers. This is also where you can offer something free or discounted to your readers for just putting in their email address.

/ Book Trailer

If you create an amazing book trailer, it could make your sales increase and create more anticipation for your release. You can decide on what type of format you would like. There are different types of styles you could go with; it could be pictures with beautiful text overlays or actors for your trailer. Having actual people in your book trailer and different scenic views could make your characters come alive and more relatable.

/ Interviews

Make a list of potential people you would like to be interviewed by. This could be a podcast of people who you already communicate with. The key to all the networking is making sure you connect with people in your field. I'm currently on a radio book tour, and every show that I have an interview on, in some way, is connected to the author industry. This ties in well with a guest blog post.

/ Speaking Engagements

Check out any conferences or events that you think you may be able to speak at. In the event that you are unable to reach out to send a proposal or get in contact with the event coordinators, attend the event and make sure you have your tools to be able to network. I suggest arriving at the event one to two hours early. Write down who you would like to talk to and have your elevator pitch ready. Also, mention that you would love to speak at the next conference. Make yourself memorable.

/ Market Price

Check out similar books in your genre to see what they are selling for. You don't want to overprice it, so be prepared to drop your price just a little bit if you don't see a big reaction in the sales. You can always use Kindle Unlimited and use their free book promotion, or discounted price tools. If you are working on a series of any kind, non-fiction or fiction, make sure that the next book is ready—or at least the first couple of chapters are done—so that your readers are not waiting for the new book in a year.

/ Order Fulfillment

This is when you need to decide if you will have Amazon fulfill your books, or if you will prepare and ship everything yourself. This includes downloads for your digital content and mailing out books for your readers. If you were to choose using your website, you would keep 100 percent of your royalties; as for going through different sources,

How to Self-Publish for Under $100

like Amazon and print-on-demand companies, you get a percentage. On Amazon, your percentage range from 30-70 percent, which in return is not much at all of a profit to you.

/ Plan

You need to plan how long each step will take and create a schedule. Timing for the promotion of your book needs to be at the right time. Things to take into consideration are: how long will editing take? When does a blog need your content for their calendar? You don't want to get people too excited about your launch too early.

/ Execute

Now that you have gone through these suggestions, you can choose which one will work for your launch. Create your own timeline of events and get ready for scheduling your deadlines. Make sure you stay on track so that things run smoothly. I always say plan for setbacks—that way when they come around, you can attack them with a positive attitude. Make sure your goals for you launch are realistic.

/ Tips for Promotion on Social Media

I love using sponsored ads because you can create your target audience and area to your readers and new readers like them. I suggest spending a few bucks to test sponsored ads. Once you get to a point where the ads are turning into sales, you will then be able to boost your budget in this area once your book is released.

Change your profile picture on your social media accounts to your book cover on release day. It takes a few seconds to change it, and ask your friends and family or readers to change their profile picture as well. This will help you get more visibility on the web for new areas and readers. Having a short but effective author bio can create a nice buzz for yourself. Having professional pictures and headshots can also add to your brand. If you have a friend or family member who is trying to create a photography portfolio, this would be a good time to ask them to do your headshots, and in return you let them use your photos and refer their business.

An author logo for your book cover or your website is highly recommended. You can use one of the services mentioned throughout this book.

Your tagline is almost like your mission statement, and it sets you apart from the competition.

The whole marketing process won't cost much at all. The most you will spend will be on your sponsored ads if that's the route you choose, and getting some marketing tools to start with.

Now that you have your marketing tools all outlined, you're ready to move on into the next phase of choosing what services are right for you when it comes to becoming a self-published author. In the next couple of chapters, I will talk about the different types of publishing sites and tools. I'll list the pros and cons and even include some good information from authors who have gone this route.

Marketing will be the way you gain your confidence. You have to set your goals and make sure you have a checklist so that things will run smoothly. It's okay if you don't use every step, but I want you to know that using most of these steps will help you to achieve a great amount of feedback and support as an author.

Make marketing a high priority on your list, and stick to a plan. The hard work will be extremely rewarding once the ball starts rolling.

Worksheet

Creating Your Marketing Plan Checklist

Dates for conferences:

○ ....

○ ....

○ ....

○ ....

○ ....

○ ....

○ ....

○ ....

Potential podcasts:

☐ ....

☐ ....

☐ ....

☐ ....

☐ ....

☐ ....

☐ ....

☐ ....

☐ ....

☐ ....

☐ ....

People to get in contact with:

- ☐ ....
- ☐ ....
- ☐ ....
- ☐ ....
- ☐ ....
- ☐ ....
- ☐ ....
- ☐ ....
- ☐ ....
- ☐ ....
- ☐ ....

// Chapter 7: Book Formatting

Formatting:

the inside format for your book to make sure the appearance has good quality and it's appealing to the eye. Margins and paragraphs are a big part of this process.

A self-published author is up against a lot of competition. The industry is constantly growing, and you want to find ways to continue to stand out and have your book look as professional as possible. I'm here to give you some great formatting types that will help you catch the eyes of new readers.

First, I want to start off with some formatting mistakes that are most common. I want you to cross these off your to-do list and never look at them again:

1. Hard Indents
2. Double Space After Periods
3. Using Copy & Paste Instead of Place
4. Quotes Instead of Apostrophes
5. Overusing Hyphens and Exclamation Points

Get out of the habit of using the tab button for indents. Use your paragraph tab to create the structure you need for your book. Double spaces after periods are like a typewriter memory, but we aren't really using a typewriter anymore, so this is a habit that you want to break. It'll be even better if you never start. So, what if you choose the format your e-book after you have finished your paperback? You want to take everything from the paperback to the e-book. Don't copy and paste—you will lose every single piece of format or italics that you included in your book. Copy and place help you control how things look when you finally add them to a new page or screen. Make sure you're using quotes when you are referring to someone's dialogue. Use apostrophes in the possessive form. Make sure you are not hyphenating compound words. This is a big no-no. Just don't do it. I hope that you cross this section out in the book with a big, red "do not use sign."

Now, let's get you on the ball to formatting your book to stand out. I want to tell you that I absolutely love the table of contents in a book. It helps to provide stability and show that you are organized. If someone just wants to read the sections about frogs one day and then the section about farm animals the next day, having a clear and straightforward table of contents will be a life saver. In an e-book, I suggest you have a clickable table of contents so that it will be easy to guide through chapters with the click of a button.

I know I went ahead of myself, but a table of contents is usually where I spend most of my time in a book. If it's a very informational book, you may also include a glossary at the end.

I feel your first few pages need to be very professional and neat when it comes to a paperback or hardcover book. Start with your title page, your copyright information, your dedication, and then—you guessed it—your table of contents. This will bring that professional look to your self-published book.

Also, when you are writing your book, make sure all of your text starts at the same place on each page. You want the text indents and paragraph to be the same throughout your book. In your e-book, this stage is important. Amazon has a feature where people can look inside your book. So you want to get to Chapter One a little bit faster, so they can read a sneak peek.

Every single one of my books all end with vital information. Sometimes it's a letter from me or it's my acknowledgments. I like to include my author photo. This is not a selfie. It's a professional headshot. If you have a friend of the family who can provide you with two are three poses for a head shot, I say go with that. Having a photo lets people get to know you as an actual person. Having a short bio to accompany your picture helps to create a lasting relationship between you and the reader.

Adding every single one of your books at the end with information on how they can purchase them is a great way to continue to create sales as your bookshelf grows. You can always change this easily when you create e-books and paperbacks by self-publishing. Having your website and all of your social media information located at the back of your book will give your readers a chance to reach out to you. This opens the floor for discussions and book club opportunities. Learning to format your own books is as simple as a Google search. Most self-publishing sites offer templates that are designed based off of their upload specifics. Sometimes they are blank, and sometimes they come formatted with default text, and then you just add your words in. Most of the self-publishing sites I know have a forum where you can discuss with other self-publishers like yourself for tips and tricks. There are free e-book templates out there that help you to create a very professional e-book for your Kindle, Nook, or even Smashwords.

I suggest that if you are having a hard time formatting your book to look on Fiverr. I recommend not spending more than $20 to get your book formatted. Learning to do it yourself will help you save money in the long run.

Learning how to do things and perfect them in the self-publishing world will help you budget. It's a full-time job, and the more skills and knowledge you have, your product will have so much more quality.

Metadata:

a set of data that describes and gives information about other data.

The times of walking around in bookstores are getting slimmer, and the ability to find just about anything online is becoming more and more popular. Making sure your book has all the correct information it needs to be found on the first page of Google, even just by typing in your name, is important. You want your metadata to be updated and as accurate as possible. We all know it's easy to do a quick search online, then walk to a bookstore. Whether you still visit local bookstores or buy books online, being able to search for your book should be an easy task. Being self-published, you have to make sure that all of your information mirrors each other.

While metadata is very simple, it can be one of the most important pieces of your book. Here are four of the most important parts of your book:

- Title
- Subtitle
- Author
- BISAC

Your title should be the main name of your book. Your subtitle could be a description to explain what your book is about, or what's in your book. Your subtitle should also include whether it's a guidebook or handbook. Your author name needs to be visible, whether it is a pen name or your full name. Learning SEO (Search Engine Optimization) to help with choosing the right keywords for your book is valuable as well. When you're choosing your book title, checking to make sure there isn't a title similar will help with your marketing. Having a book that is very close to your title can hinder your book's visibility.

Other important data that is part of your book are:

- ISBN: $0-1000
- Format: $5-75
- Pub Date

Your ISBN is a number assigned to your book. We will discuss more about ISBNs in the next section. The format is the type of format your book is in, whether it be paperback, audio, or e-book. Your pub date is the date that your book was published or is going to be released. Most of the information above is in the simplest form. These are items you should always keep track of. Metadata is very important, and its worth making sure that the documentation for this is always correct.

When people start to search for your book, they will find it by the information you include when you are uploading your book to your self-publishing site of choice. If this information isn't accurate, the chances of someone searching and finding your book is not very high. For example, if you were addressing your book by the subtitle and not the title, and if someone was to go look it up by the subtitle and you didn't include the subtitle when you were uploading your book, that information for that particular book will not show up. Hopefully, you remember to fill in all these fields. Especially the one marked author.

- Category (BISAC)
- Description
- Target Audience

These items help to set your book apart from other books in the same category. If your book stands out by a subtitle but has the same main idea of another book, your book has the chance to be seen first. Making sure to choose the correct category for your book will make or break your sales. You can't have a book about kittens in the puppy section. Because you chose to include your book in the small animals category, your book will get lost in those searches. Having a clear and accurate description of your book that gives a nice outline—but not gives too much away—is also a way to get a reader intrigued. Knowing your target audience will help you become more discoverable in those certain category searches.

Knowing how important metadata is of your book's success, we can move on to thinking like a reader. When you go to search for an item, you usually write short phrases that are about three to four words. So, when you are typing to choose keywords for your book, you should search for words that you would look up to find your book. Here is an example for this book—people will most likely search for: how to self-publish, self-publishing on a budget, or self-publishing a book.

When you're using keywords, you have to think like your readers and make sure you choose the most fitting ones. Once you master your metadata and find your perfect keywords, you have the master key to be discovered online by many readers. This will also help your rankings and, of course, you want to be at the top of the search engine page when the results come up.

Other items for metadata describes things like your book size, page count, and who the book is published by. This task may seem like it is self-explanatory, but no matter how tedious the task is, making sure everything in these sections is done correctly will save you lots of time. Don't do it the wrong way the first time—trust me I know. You don't want your book to rank 3,484,237 for a whole year because you put your book in the wrong category and used keywords that made no sense.

I'd like to share my five steps to make sure you are able to check off this task with confidence:

1. Have a list of three to five keywords and phrases
2. Create a file with all your metadata
3. Make sure that every field identified above is filled out correctly when uploading your book
4. Use your file every time you fill out any information about your book
5. When you learn new stuff, update your metadata

Library of Congress - The Preassigned Control Number (PCN) program assigns a Library of Congress Control Number to titles most likely to be acquired by the Library of Congress as well as some other categories of books.

Books that do exceptionally well in the library are in the lines of self-help and historical fiction. Wanting to get a book like this in the library will require you to have a registered Library of Congress number. The first thing that you want to know is that getting a number is free. This process should take no longer than two to three days, and you can get a response back via email. You have your ISBN number in order to obtain an LCN. The website is www.LOC.gov; you will need to create an account and follow the instructions on how to sign up for your LCN. Once you get your email from them, you will need to save this number for your records. Having this number helps you to exist in libraries all over the world.

TIP: You can donate your book or books to the library to be added to the shelves. This is a bonus because donations are a great tax deduction when it's time to file your taxes.

ISBN: a 13-digit number assigned by standard book numbering agencies to control and facilitate activities within the publishing industry.

You may have seen ISBN-10 or ISBN-13. These two numbers are used for the same thing, but ISBN-10 is used for books published before 2007. ISBN-13 is used for books published after January 1, 2007. If you want to self-publish, you must have an ISBN number. This number helps to track your book if you were to come out with a different edition.

I had to change my ISBNs for my books when I decided to change the interior and the cover of my first two books. This process wasn't hard because I used a free and assigned ISBN by CreateSpace. That leads me to the next section.

The cost of an ISBN number can range anywhere from $100 to $1000. Most of the self-published sites do give you a free ISBN if you have plans on always being a self-published author and never selling your work. This is the most cost-efficient way to go. It just means that if you were approached by a publishing company, you could not sell the rights to your book to them because CreateSpace gave you the ISBN. If you want to always own your book and not have to worry, this would be something you would want to work in your budget somehow. If you could only spend a certain amount on your first book, and then you take your royalties from that to pay for Part II of your next book's ISBN, you can still make this work in your favor. If you want to know more information about how ISBNs work, check out Bowker at www.bowker.com.

You do not need an ISBN if you plan to solely sell your books face-to-face. If you want your book online, or if you want them in every store, you most definitely need an ISBN.

Worksheet

Metadata Information

Title: ....

Subtitle: ....

Author: ....

Category: ....

Format: ....

Pub Date: ....

Target Audience: ....

ISBN: ....

Description: ....

Title: ....

Subtitle: ....

Author: ....

Category: ....

Format: ....

Pub Date: ....

Target Audience: ....

ISBN: ....

Description ....

....

....

....

....

Title: ....

Subtitle: ....

Author: ....

Category: ....

Format: ....

Pub Date: ....

Target Audience: ....

ISBN: ....

Description: ....

....

....

....

....

Title: ....

Subtitle: ....

Author: ....

Category: ....

Format: ....

Pub Date: ....

Target Audience: ....

ISBN: ....

Description: ....

....

....

....

....

Title: ....

Subtitle: ....

Author: ....

Category: ....

Format: ....

Pub Date: ....

Target Audience: ....

ISBN: ....

Description: ....

....

....

....

....

Title: ....

Subtitle: ....

Author: ....

Category: ....

Format: ....

Pub Date: ....

Target Audience: ....

ISBN: ....

Description: ....

....

....

....

....

// Chapter 8: KDP

KDP:

One of the fastest and free ways to help authors and publishers to keep control and publish their books within the Amazon Bookstore.

KDP Select:

creates a new way for authors to include their titles into the Kindle Owner's Library.

We've gone through the important steps of what to do to get you started with your book, and now you need to decide which self-publishing platform you will choose to publish your book. In the next few chapters, you'll learn about publishing your e-book and paperbacks online.

Like all the self-publishing vehicles that are available, KDP offers some pros and cons. The first thing you'll notice upon going the KDP route is that it provides you with a "bookshelf" that shows you an overview of your e-books and paperbacks all in one spot. You can edit your book details and see what sales channels your books have been sold in—meaning you can see your US, UK, and Japan sales. You can see the pages read and you can see how many books have been purchased. I love seeing my earnings, because it motivates me month-to-month to make sure I'm staying up on my marketing strategies.

In a nutshell, KDP provides your full book sales month-to-month in an easy to navigate interface.

/ What is it?

I decided to start with KDP because it's the most popular self-publishing platform right now. Amazon has created a massive digital book catalog of books, from established authors to thousands of newly self-published authors. KDP has given authors a way to publish their work for free while keeping it easy and convenient.

When I decided to self-publish, I was mainly concerned about how to publish a paperback book. I was really obsessed with just feeling a book in my hands. Once I went through the paperback upload through CreateSpace, it led me to

KDP. This was new to me. Although I've read numerous books on Amazon Kindle, I never would have thought that I could publish my own books on Amazon.

This opened a whole new avenue of residual income for me. Knowing your resources and how to use them is what helps a self-published author when it's time to publish.

I'll give you all the tools your book should include. You have your metadata and your valuable marketing guide. Now it's time to prepare and upload your book.

/ How does it work?

There are no upfront charges to self-publish with KDP. Simply, you choose your own list price, check off the corresponding fields, fill out the metadata, and submit.

/ Cost

However, that does not mean that there aren't any finances to consider. While there are no upfront fees to self-publish, what you choose in regards to availability directly affect your bottom line. They provide the options of 35 percent and 70 percent for your royalty payment.

/ KDP Select

KDP Select allows readers to read your books for free. Amazon has created a special fund to compensate the authors who decide to use this method. KDP Select, along with Kindle Unlimited, offers a way where you can run promotions and discounted sales of your books. Your book will not be automatically added to this option. You have to opt-in. You can choose to re-enroll every ninety days or stay enrolled indefinitely. You have five free promotion days. You own complete control over your work.

/ Pros

Exposure for your books will increase being in this program. For example, a free book promotion for two days can increase sales if you have a series. Book 1 is free; if the reader liked it, he will purchase Book 2.

Compensation for having your book be a part of the lending library can be very rewarding, or you could barely see any change at all. If you are one of the lucky authors whose book has been borrowed or downloaded over a million times, you could get a check from the KDP Select fund that goes by the pages read in that month. They have a scale from Top 1-100 authors with bonuses starting from $1,000 to $25,000.

Duration of KDP Select lasts about ninety days. The option to stay enrolled or not to enroll for the next ninety days is up to the author.

Enrolling your book can create more visibility in the "Customers Who Bought This Item Also Bought" section.

/ Cons

You give up the rights to sell your book anywhere but Amazon. KDP Select means that you are selling exclusively on Amazon for ninety days. If you are selling more books on other platforms or on your website, KDP Select may not be the right option for you. If during the Select time you want to end it, you can't. You'll have to fulfill the remainder of the ninety days regardless of how sales are going.

If the digital version of your book appears to be available for pre-order, for sale, or for free elsewhere (such as on your website or blog, or a third party's website), then it is not eligible for KDP Select.

If you don't comply with KDP Select's terms and conditions, you will not receive your royalties for the digital book. They can also withhold payments of all your digital books for a period of up to ninety days while they investigate. Probation is also a part of your future participation in KDP Select or KDP.

Because Amazon Prime members love low-priced books, your book that's below $5.99 may not get borrowed much. Lots of readers like to use their borrowing ability on a New York Times Best Seller list. This is another chance you take. It's a possibility that you will make less than ten cents in your first thirty days.

/ E-book/Paperback

KDP just rolled out beta testing of producing an option for their publisher to upload their e-book and paperback book on the same platform. Before this change in October 2016, KDP referred all of their paperback sales to CreateSpace, whom they endorsed.

/ Mistakes

The biggest mistakes I see here when getting ready to publish a book on KDP is a book in the wrong category. This would make it hard for your book to sell and reach the Best-Seller Top 100 list if you released in the wrong category. This can be changed, but it takes 24-72 hours for this change to take effect. That's three days of sales you could be missing out on. So, it's best you double check—triple check, even—all of the information you are providing when uploading your book.

Tips

/ KDP Paperback

Paperbacks as a part of your face-to-face sales is a very good idea. You need paperbacks for a book signing, and just to pitch at any given time. Having KDP now offer paperbacks on their website saves time, and it helps to keep all your sales in one place. Lots of people enjoy different genres, and different age groups either enjoy having a book they can feel or a book they can read when convenient. I still buy paperback books, because sometimes you just need it in your hand.

/ Distribution

Your paperback book will be distributed in the US, Europe, and Japan, through the Amazon sales channel. I love having the option to have Amazon fulfill shipments for me, because then it's less work. When readers request a signed copy, I usually provide an upgrade on this service; I'll use a book I have on hand, and I'll be responsible for shipping materials and shipping cost.

/ Royalties

You can earn up to 60 percent of royalties off of your set list price. Printing cost will be deducted from this total. I love when people price their work with confidence. Writing anywhere below 50,000 words, I suggest $10 and below. Anything that is 50K and above, I would suggest $10 and above. This way, you are still making a good amount of residual income from your paperbacks. Sometimes it does better on your website than it does on Amazon.
You still maintain creative control over your work—still remember to get your work under copyright. Having on-demand printing means your work will never be out of stock. You can always order more books, and your readers will never see the sold out icon.

The best thing about using KDP for Kindle and paperbacks is that it's completely free. When you get to this step, you can choose to publish with a free ISBN, create your own cover, and select your own price.

Leading up to this process, the only thing you will have to worry about is your author photo, your synopsis, book blurb, metadata, and getting your book edited.

In the next chapter, you will learn about another print-on-demand self-publishing company that caters to paperbacks.

// Chapter 9: CreateSpace

Through this service, you can sell books for a fraction of the cost of traditional manufacturing, while maintaining more control over your materials. CreateSpace makes it simple to distribute your books, whether it's on retail outlets, your website or other bookstores and facilities.

CreateSpace is one of the top self-publishing platforms. Being able to have your book uploaded directly to Amazon, available to libraries, and in the CreateSpace e-store makes selling your book easier. You still have to put your marketing to work, but this is a free and easy platform.

Deciding on self-publishing is a big decision that you have chosen to make. I have to let you know again that this route takes a lot of work and research. You have to stay on top of things, and if you are doing it on your $100 budget, you have to triple check your work at all times. I want to go over a few pros and cons with you when it comes to CreateSpace.

/ Pros

You can have your book on one of the latest online retailers, which is Amazon. Your book has the potential to sell in several countries. A larger audience where millions of new visitors come daily can give you a chance to make sales. This also depends on your metadata and how you categorize your book.

Self-publishing through CreateSpace can help you to get 40 percent to 70 percent royalties. When you are signed to a traditional publishing company, this rate is sometimes non-negotiable. A traditional publishing company can give you cents for every book sold versus a percentage. It just depends on the type of contract you sign. With print-on-demand, you have options to up-charge your book and pocket your royalties.

I love that you can provide discounts on your books and still make a decent profit. I know that the goal when you're self-publishing is to have more visibility, but you have the option to not sell your books on Amazon and solely create face-to-face sales at whatever markup price you decide.

CreateSpace makes it easy for you to publish a book with guided steps. You can easily access the cover creator and download templates to format your book.

The print-on-demand service can serve as a drop ship for you to send books directly to your customers from CreateSpace. It saves you time and money with shipping and packaging.

/ Cons

Your first time uploading a book to CreateSpace may bring some difficulties, like some of the vocabulary. You already have to fill out the site information for your book, but you will come across and learn new terminology, things like the trim size and marginal formatting. Not knowing what these terms mean can certainly discourage you. This stage can make a new author very confused. CreateSpace offers different services, but being on a tight budget, those services can seem relatively expensive.

It may take you a few times to upload your book correctly once it goes through the proofing section. I will tell you this: how your book looks on the online proofer is exactly how it will print. It will pick up every simple mistake you make while formatting your book.

When you self-publish on Amazon, your book gets thrown into this big sea of hope, and you just hope you don't sink. New books are being added every second to Amazon by self-published authors. The competition has gotten more competitive as self-publishing continues to become more popular.

It's a little harder to get customer information when using these third party sites to sell books. If you were to provide your paperbacks on your own website, you would be able to collect customer information for future promotions.

Another con is that with your discounts and promotions, you have limited resources with this in the CreateSpace e-store. With Kindle, you would have to be enrolled in KDP Select to have certain promotions.

I honestly love CreateSpace, and once I create a larger following of avid readers I will eventually invest in my own ISBN. I will continue to publish them with CreateSpace so that I exclusively own all the rights to my books. I wanted to get an opinion from another customer who also happens to be from Australia to share some of her pros and cons with you about publishing in another country:

/ CreateSpace pros and cons from an Australian Author*

CreateSpace is brilliant for self-published writers like myself. I'm an Australian romance author and have been working with CreateSpace since 2015.

I have found CreateSpace easy to work with, and their customer service is excellent. On the few occasions I have needed help, they have replied promptly via email within 24 hours. Because of the time differences between the US and Australia, I'm always thankful when help is at hand via email.

When I started looking at printing my books, I found the costs too high in Melbourne, Australia, and considered both IngramSpark and CreateSpace. I didn't like the setup costs for IngramSpark and felt that it outweighed the benefits they offer. Plus, each time you make changes to your book on IngramSpark, you have to pay anther setup the cost. From time-to-time, they have specials when it's free to do this, but the special may not be available when you need to make the changes.

When I started out, I made mistakes with editing and uploading, and CreateSpace allows you to upload your cover and/or manuscript multiple times without any (cost) penalty.

CreateSpace allows me to sell my paperbacks to a worldwide market (i.e.: outside of Australia) at a reasonable cost via Amazon and their own CreateSpace sales platform.

However, the downside is that I can't access US libraries and other US stores because I use my own ISBN rather than use theirs.

Personally, I think this is unfair of CreateSpace in restricting my sales. If you don't use their ISBNs, then you don't have access to their libraries and academic institutions' channels. I don't want to use their ISBN because I want to own my own ISBN. The ISBN is an individual number which recognizes books as belonging to an author. This is particularly important as I now sell my books to Australian and New Zealand libraries. I would not be able to do this without my own ISBN.

The quality of their printing is very good and the pricing is very reasonable. What is expensive is the shipping to Australia. The costs are very high, especially when ordering a proof book and translating US dollars into Australian. For this reason, I have now actively sought out an Australian printer and finally found one where the quality is comparable, but the shipping costs are substantially cheaper. As a self-published writer, I am mindful of each dollar I spend.

However, I will use CreateSpace when I need to ship within the US, as their pricing is affordable. For example, I have on occasion donated books and sent them via CreateSpace within the US.

The downsides of CreateSpace are:

- Shipping costs to Australia
- Restricting sales through channels if you don't use their ISBN
- As an Australian, I have to be paid by check (not direct debit), so I lose a lot of royalties in bank fees, and the minimum payment amount is /£100/€100.

The upsides of CreateSpace are:

- Easy to navigate website
- Brilliant customer service
- Quality printing
- Linking to Amazon

How has CreateSpace helped me with sales?

- They have made it super easy for me to print books and have them delivered to Australia
- The book quality is excellent and readers are happy to purchase my books
- I can print small or large quantities which helps with cost
- I can post books, within the US, for competitions and charities, and their costings are reasonable (and much cheaper than posting from Australia)
- I have been able to increase and expand my brand awareness to the US, UK, and Europe

Despite the cons of CreateSpace, I would definitely recommend using them even if you are restricted with sales.

As a multi-published writer, I firmly believe that authors should own their ISBNs. Here in Australia, we have to pay for them. But despite the cost, I encourage writers to do so, as it links our books to us, not a company.

This information was correct at the time of submission.

- Joanne Dannon
www.joannedannon.com

CreateSpace is a great tool for getting started. If you want to be able to publish a book and just get it out to people in your community and family, it's a great place to start. If you want to take your craft serious and start to get feedback, CreateSpace helps you to get to that next step as well. All of the research and hard, tedious work is worth it. Holding your book in your hand will give you so much joy. I hope you have an amazing experience with whichever self-publishing company you choose.

// Chapter 10: IngramSpark

From print-on-demand to e-book publishing, IngramSpark makes getting your content to readers easy.

With IngramSpark, I want to jump into the noticeable things that are clearly different with this site. They have a setup fee. I would almost put this in a pay-for-publishing category, because you are basically paying a fee to get started with this website. Don't count them out just yet, though, because we have a lot to discuss to see if this is the right service for you. Of course, IngramSpark caters to small volume customers and the self-publishing community.

When starting your IngramSpark journey, you can choose to publish e-books, paperbacks, or you can decide to do digital and print together.

Here is a list of all the things included in your setup fee:

- Self-Publishing Guide
- File Creation Guide
- Partner Discounts
- EPUB Conversion Options
- E-Reader Capability
- 65+ Trim Sizes
- Hardback or Paperback
- Black & White
- Color, Premium Options
- Gloss or Matte
- Global Distribution Access to 39,000 Retailers and Libraries
- Distribution Access to 80+ Online Retailers
- Amazon
- Kobo
- Nook
- iBooks Store, and more.
- Flexible Deliveries
- Multiple Currencies for More Sales and Opportunities
- Advanced Reports
- Self-Publishing Tools
- Advertising and Marketing Channels

Publishing through IngramSpark:

- Books are distributed through Ingram, which is what stores use to order books
- Books are returnable, which means stores are much more likely to stock your book
- Title set up is $49, but this fee is waived if you order 50+ copies of your book within sixty days of setup
- During the title setup, you enter the publication date. Once you approve your files, IngramSpark puts your book on preorder until that publication date.

That list is certainly long for all of the benefits you receive once you pay a one-time setup fee. Before we move on, I just want you to know that IngramSpark also owns Lighting Source.

The one-time fee may be one time, but as you will soon learn, there are other expenses and purchases necessary once you get the ball rolling. The only thing that seems to make the cost so you continue to pay is that if you order at least fifty books in the first sixty days, your $49 fee can be refunded. Here is a list of other fees, etc.:

/ Fees for Set Up & Revenues

Print costs and print options mirror what Lightening Source has:

- $49 cost to setup paperbacks and e-books
- $49 cost for paperback only setup
- $25 cost for e-books only setup
- $49 refunded if fifty copy runs ordered by publisher within sixty days
- $12 annual fee per title
- No proof cost (if .pdf)
- $25 revision fee once in distribution channels
- 55% locked discount (on list price) to retailers— Spark might revise this following publisher feedback
- 45% publisher revenue on list price after deduction of print manufacturing costs
- 40% publisher revenue on e-books

I love including stories from people who have tried these sites and can offer you real-life experience along with my hard facts. Here is an Australian author who uses IngramSpark, and she breaks down her experience for you.

When I first started writing my book, Orgasm Unleashed: Your Guide to Pleasure, Healing and Power, I had a few goals:

Finish the book in three months.

I wanted the most important information I'd gathered over the years to be in one place, so if I died the day after it was published, this knowledge would be accessible to everyone. To use the book not just to help people or make a profit, but to start a movement and to open doors for my business. Obviously, goal number one was a little ambitious. As a first-time author and generally busy guy, it ended up taking me two years to complete my book. However, the second and third goals were achieved, in large part due to IngramSpark's self-publishing.

I can now "die happy," as they say, as my work is out there, and has already changed the lives of thousands of women, and I hope will continue to help thousands more.

I am also now able to use my book not only as an income stream, but as a business card, gift, deal sweetener, and conversation starter with potential clients. As an added bonus, I was even a best-seller on Amazon's best-sellers lists for a couple of days!

I've had a great run with IngramSpark. Out of the thousands of books I've had printed so far, I've only seen one misprint. While the ordering system is a little clunky, it's generally easy to make orders and send them wherever they need to go straight from the publishers. No double handling is a big plus.

One thing I will say is, get someone else to sort out your book's formatting, for both the text and the cover. If you are a whiz at these things, then sure, you sort it out, but for the rest of us, just pay someone. You can find plenty of low-cost designers and editors online, and that's fine; just find someone who knows what they are doing. You want to get it right the first time. IngramSpark does not offer proofreading, editing, design, or anything else like that. It's a double-edged sword—what you send into print is exactly what you get.

Another tip I have for someone starting out with them is to get organized and make orders ahead of time, as both the printing and postage are much cheaper if you can just wait that extra week or so for delivery. If you need an order in a hurry, it's still affordable. However, as any small business person knows, that if you can decrease your overheads easily, do it.

While publishing a book hasn't drastically changed my business or profits in and of itself, it is definitely an important piece of my overall offerings, and IngramSpark has helped make that possible.

I'm trying to start a movement, a new sexual revolution. And while this movement is only in the beginning stages—and I don't know if I'll ever write a book again—I know that even in putting out this information that I have in my book, I've already changed the world for the better.

What are your plans for your book? Write it down. Look at the content. Now, think bigger. Books can be so much more than just a good read, or even an income stream. How is your book going to get your gift to the world? What is your mission in life? How will this book help you achieve that?

One more tip I'd like to offer is to have a team. Writing a book is a big deal, and can take a huge chunk of time, energy, and resources. Gather a good team around you, not just friends, but a good editor, designer, business coaches, mentors, and most importantly, you. Make sure that you are on board 100 percent. This is your mission, your gift. You are the leader of this expedition, so lead.

-Eyal Matsliah

There are some disadvantages of getting started with IngramSpark. You may end up shelling out more money than you want to just trying to initiate the process. If you don't have your document formatted the right way the first time, you may have to pay another fee to upload it again. I would hire someone who is excellent at IngramSpark files to help you with this, someone who can offer multiple revisions or a refund if the files aren't accepted on upload. After all, that's why you are paying them.

You can choose from two different royalty payouts which are a 55 percent option and 40 percent payout. IngramSpark gets a lot of rave reviews for its quality and lightweight books when you receive your proofs. This helps with the cost of postage.

I love the option that IngramSpark's provides which allows you to accept returns from bookstores that you choose. The hard thing about this and being a self-published author is the cost you may inquire if a store purchases your books and they don't sell. This will leave you with a fee and used book that has been shipped multiple times.

I don't want to include all of this information to scare you because you need to know. IngramSpark is very professional, and has a lot to offer. This wouldn't be the go-to site I would choose for a new author. As we know, sales aren't guaranteed off of your very first book. I would suggest this platform to a mid-level selling indie author who can bring in at least 5,000 sells or more on first day releases.

I love leaving you all with this information you can use when you make your decision, so we will look further into the pros and cons and things that IngramSpark can offer you.

All in all, IngramSpark is a very good candidate for publishing your book. This is a more expensive option, and if you are trying to produce your book for under $100, you may want to save this option for further along in your career, or once you receive your royalties from sales of your first book. IngramSpark is like graduating to the next level because you mastered the beginner level of becoming an author.

// Chapter 11: Vanity Publishing

A company that charges an author to publish a book.
Offering the option for the author to also purchase the book
or books is also an example of Vanity Publishing.
Vanity publishing is still around even though self-publishing
is well on the rise. Authors can choose to have their books
published by paying for publishing as the option. If you're
not sure what vanity publishing is, here are a few terms that
companies have used to describe it:

- Joint Venture Publishing
- Co-Operative Publishing
- Subsidy Publishing
- Shared Responsibility Publishing

With so much controversy surrounded around vanity publishing, there is one thing I must get out of the way. Vanity publishing is not SELF-PUBLISHING. With self-publishing, you task out things like editing, book covers, and graphics, and you pay for those services. In the end, you are the primary source of your book and your finances. You will receive all royalties. With vanity publishing, you are paying someone to publish your book. Contracts will be involved, and you will probably negotiate a percentage of your royalties. I never want you to be confused by these terms. We will dig a little deeper on this subject and break down pros and cons to help you understand all that vanity publishing entails.

/ Examples of Vanity Publishing

- Being told you need to purchase thousands of copies of your book once it's done
- If you are going into debt trying to publish a book with a company
- Believing that you can publish a book just because, and it will sell
- If you think your book is fantastic and you need no marketing or plans (you're a little delusional at this point)

These are all examples of stepping into vanity publishing.

Note that a real publishing company would not ask you to
pay for anything up front. A publishing company who has
an interest in you will not ask you to pay because they feel
your work is good enough to make money. If you are asked
to pay for your titles to be published, my advice is to run!
Self-publish right away. I'll give you a few reasons why
someone is asking you to pay or why you were rejected by a
publishing company:

- Your pitch may have not been professional
- You need to work on your approach
- Collect stats for website
- Your story may not be ready
- Your writing skills still need work
- Timing

These are not things that should discourage you, though,
because it's a hurdle that many new authors face. Some
established authors who are familiar–none–probably didn't
get started as soon as you did. Some authors who have
been writing for years and still haven't reached that goal of
x amount of books sold. Some probably never had a best-
seller. Don't ever get discouraged to the point where you feel
you need to pay someone to publish your work.

I'll say this one thing that I love about self-publishing: I have
all the rights to my work. I can continuously update it with

new information, or even go back and edit my covers or my author photo on the back—because it's mine, and I own every right to it. It may take a little time, but I will have creative control over my books for the rest of my life.

Now, if you happen to approach a vanity publishing company and your work is top-notch, and you know you have the skills to be published, I suggest you submit your book like crazy to publishing companies who won't ask you to pay. No matter how good or bad your work is. It's sad to say, but a vanity publishing company will still ask you to pay. They charge you an upfront cost, and if your book doesn't sell, they still have the fee and profit off of you. You may not even get quality editing or an overview of your book from the company, because they have no expectations for your book.

/ When You Should Use Vanity Publishing

There is always an exception to all things that many say no to. I, for one, say everything has a chance to be great. If you view writing as a hobby and you won't go broke, vanity publishing is probably for you.

I would just make sure my book is edited and formatted correctly even if the vanity company provides this service. If you're not in it for the money and you really just want to have your name on a book to see on your shelf, go the vanity publishing route. It's your money, and you have a right to choose, and this is only fair that I mentioned this as an option.

Note that you probably won't make the money that you spent back.

/ Advantages

- Keep exclusive rights to your work
- Creative control
- Cover design (possibly for a small fee)
- You can publish whatever you want that may be rejected by a traditional publisher
- Disadvantages
- You took a risk and paid for publishing, and your book may not sell
- Possibly starting your career as an author in debt
- Run into issues with wholesalers for copies of your book
- Being labeled as a vanity publishing author (especially if it's a well-known company)

Vanity publishing to me makes more sense for niche writers who are writing niche-based books that provide in-depth information. Again, it probably started as a hobby, and they just want to be published.

The problem with this is I want my content creators to keep the money that they have made and put it back into their business. The whole purpose of this book is to talk about everything and being transparent about the writing industry. I want you to be able to choose for yourself. I give you all of this information so that ultimately you can make your own decision.

With everything that goes into these businesses, there are always pros and cons.

The fact that vanity publishing is referred to as the "switch and bait" makes me cringe.

People often confuse vanity publishing with all the names it is associated with listed above. But all in all, they all have the same business model. They are all fee-charging companies. All companies will claim to be better than a traditional publishing company or another vanity publishing company, but will ultimately provide the same things.

Here is a list of a few common vanity publishing companies that you should know:

- Commonwealth Publications
- Northwest Publications
- Sovereign Publishing
- Minerva Press Ltd.
- Vantage Press

How to spot a Vanity Publishing Company

- A setup fee or deposit
- Fees for printing or publication
- Extra service fees
- Fees are a part of every cost
- Pre-purchase requirement
- Pre-sale requirement
- A sales guarantee
- Withheld royalties
- Pressure to buy x amount of books

These are all signs of being approached or that you have approached a vanity publishing company.

I suggest that you always learn about the process and stay up to date with the writing industry's new and old skills. I research every company that I want to do business with, and I look for people who have worked with them to get an overview of how much they value the working relationship. If you are a new author, this is a must for you. You must know the laws, and you must research the route you want to choose. You will be able to ask questions, but no research is better than on your own. I believe that knowledge can help you navigate any career; practicing and perfecting your craft will take you far in this industry.

Here are a few tips that I recommend you use when searching for a publishing company or researching a vanity publishing company:

- Order a book from the company to review the formatting, etc.
- Contact writers who have worked with the company
- Research the publisher
- Have someone review your contract
- Research distribution of wholesaler
- Legal contracts reviewed

With any business deal or new contract you should have someone look at it. There are warning signs that you could look for that will avoid a toll on your pockets that will cost you more. I want every inch of information in this chapter to be taken very seriously. You can use these tips for just about every aspect of your life when searching for a company of any service.

Now that you know that vanity publishing is mainly paying to publish your work, you can form your own opinion on whether this service is right for you. If you feel that you will profit from a vanity publishing company with the information you have, you can move to the next step.

If you believe that vanity publishing is not the route you want to go and that you would like more guidance and not to pay anything up front, you should try a traditional publishing company. Research and reach out. Never be afraid to revise your pitch until you get the answers you are looking for; you need to be prepared and ready for meetings at any time. You may be well aware of all your choices, and that self-publishing is the right choice for you. You have all the tools you need in this book to be successful and be creative. Now the next step is to put a plan into action.

I would never want to discourage anyone from trying a method that they feel is right for them, because the truth is someone will have success from it. It's about your preference. Knowing more and being able to access every situation beforehand is my goal here, giving you the perspective from all points of views.

In closing, I would like to add in things that a vanity publishing company probably won't tell you for a little comic relief:

A vanity publishing company won't tell you that your book is poorly edited and lacks substance. They won't inform you that the thousands of copies you are about to publish will probably sit in your trunk for years because you have no marketing plan, or any plan really. Your deposit and setup fee is non-refundable, and even if you are not satisfied with their services, you won't get your money back. You'll probably have to pay more money, often called an extra fee, to get out of your contract.

Lessons will be learned throughout this journey; writing and becoming an author is a process that won't be perfect overnight. It's like rolled oats. It has to sit and cook for a little while. Being an author isn't instant. Overnight success is possible, though, of course it is. Everyone has the potential to be viral, but that shouldn't be your goal. Your end goal should be to capture the hearts and minds of readers across the country. Be on bookshelves you never thought you would reach.

Always do your due diligence and get a second opinion.

// Chapter 12: Hybrid Publishing

Hybrid publishing:
a combination of self-publishing and traditional publishing that could be a great experience for publishers and authors

Hybrid publishing is a new dynamic that has taken the writing industry by storm. This innovative way of thinking is to help authors and publishers both get what they want out of a deal. This creates a mutual benefit for both parties involved.

If you're reading this and you've never heard of hybrid publishing, it's because it started about four years ago. When most writers think of releasing their book, the two options that come to mind are self-publishing or traditional publishing. There is an accepted assumption among new writers that there is no other route. I am here to tell you that more and more, getting your book in the hands of your readers is diversifying and changing with the landscape of how and when people read.

Hybrid publishing has slowly but surely picked up the momentum as being the new thing in the publishing world. Here are three things that will help you identify hybrid publishing:

- No Advance Pay
- Less Salaried Employees
- Marketing

You won't get any advance pay like you may (though highly unlikely) receive with big publishing companies. This does help the companies to have more money in turn to market your book and price it accordingly. During this process you can receive higher royalties, but not as high as you would with self-publishing. Hybrid publishing should not ask you to pay to be published, either.

You probably won't have an entire team. As a matter fact, the hybrid company may have lots of virtual employees who video chat, message, and email you throughout the process. This small team also has the option to accept the books that will make them money. No one wants to take on a project that will have them stuck in the negative.

Your book will probably take less than a year to come out. The demand is high and it needs to be done quickly. They can attract like-minded individuals who see your work, and in return it builds their business. By having a good turnaround time they can publish more books in a one year span. Be prepared to work and have a deadline.

The one thing that creates irony in this situation is that the books are still published through self-publishing/print-on-demand companies, like Lightning Source. If they are using a company that doesn't accept returns, you can possibly stunt the growth of your career simply by how the hybrid company chooses to print the books.

Choosing what route to go is almost like which door to choose. Most writers either started off as a self-published author, later signed a publishing deal, or started with a publishing company and learned some things and decided to self-publish. This can be considered hybrid publishing. In fact, I can consider myself a hybrid author to some extent. My journey as a self-published author has been rewarding, but I know that a publishing company who has the means and staff could take me to the next level. Every decision is based off what's best for your literary career. We can agree that the term means different things to different people, but the fact is it's meeting somewhere in the middle between self-publishing and traditional. Right now we are just going to agree that hybrid publishing is a confusing term.

Hybrid publishing has the potential to provide you a community of people who can provide you support or answer your questions. With every new or innovative wave there are drawbacks, and hybrid can fall into the same ranks of self-publishing.

When thinking about hybrid publishing, here are a few questions you should ask:

- Who's paying for it?
- Will there be a distribution pitch?
- How will the books be distributed?
- What is the editing process like?
- What is marketing and promotion like?
- Can you reach out to recent authors?

You should know off the top before you sign any contracts who is paying for this project and taking the financial risk. Know that you shouldn't have a financial obligation or expect one. Information you should look for is how many books will be printed and your sales mark for you debut.

Knowing if your publishing company has secured any pre-order sales is a must as well. You should be able to find out about the distribution pitch. Is there a marketing plan in place? These are legit questions for any author. If you are struggling with getting these questions answered, you should rethink the decision with this company. Plain and simple.

We know the main print-on-demand companies and we know how they work. If your publishing company is going this route, a conversation needs to happen. Are they providing the ISBN or settling for a free ISBN? If the goal is to sit on a physical shelf, this requires contacts and money. One thing I will say is that if your hybrid publishing company is focusing on print books, you can solely focus on having all rights to your e-book. You can sell that and earn all the royalties depending on what route you take.

You are the author, and most things you shouldn't have to worry about. But as a good, involved author, you should be involved in every single detail. If they take your manuscript without sending any changes to you this should raise a red flag. No book is ever ready for print without a few rounds of editing. This shows a lack of professionalism on their end. If there is a marketing plan in place for each one of your titles, there are questions that need to be answered. Were they sent out to test readers? Will there be a press release? If all your company does is make the title for sale without pitching or marketing months or even a year out, then you should again rethink this hybrid company.

Reaching out to any former or current authors signed with the company could help you also determine what the vibe is like. Most likely, they can give you a run down on how things worked out for them and if they were pleased with the service.

Before you sign anything, have a second pair of eyes look over your contract, and make sure you ask all the necessary questions before signing.

/Hybrid Publishing's Future

The risk is becoming greater for traditional publishing companies. New authors and aspiring writers are popping up every day trying to be a future best-seller. We have Facebook publishing companies, and writers turning down publishers who are emailing and sending contracts. The industry becomes a little cloudy when this starts to happen, and it's hard to filter out the good from the bad.

Hybrid is becoming a new way because it takes the risk off of some traditional publishing companies who don't want a financial risk with a new author. No one knows them when they don't have a social media following or a lot of readers who are proven to buy whatever they are selling.

When you self-publish, it can take time to build an audience, and that's okay. You're constantly producing quality books, and if you are sticking to a budget, you can easily put the money you make right back into your budget.

Hybrid publishing is the best fit mainly once you've self-published and have a good amount of sales and reports to show your growth. Actively promoting your work can help when you decide to take the hybrid route.

You won't have to pay for publishing and you can be involved in the process.

The future for hybrid publishing is very bright, with authors and publishing companies coming together to find that medium that will work for them. With any innovative model, there will be pros and cons. There will be horror stories and many people telling you to run the opposite way. Going into every situation with an open-mind can pave the way for massive success. Hear out the details, ask questions, and then decide for yourself.

When something doesn't work out completely and turns out the opposite way of how you had envisioned it, you can then turn around and blog or vlog about your experience to make others aware of that structure. I say always, be tasteful in your approach when it comes to reviews. Companies have the ability to change and reinvent themselves, and your word can hold lots of weight in the industry.

In conclusion, hybrid publishing is like the best of both worlds. It's the happy medium that will satisfy the publisher and author to create a win-win situation. Like all contracts, the terms are negotiated. The end goal should to always try to build your audience to create connections and make money. The route you choose shouldn't define your career, because everyone starts somewhere.

As a result of this industry forever changing, there will be more companies popping up defining themselves as hybrid publishing. The rise of Facebook publishers and writers turned agents are already at a record high number.
My fair warning to you is to never be so eager to say yes to just anything and anybody. Take some time to read, and research reviews.

// Conclusion

You have officially picked my brain. I have shared so much information with you that you will be successful in your self-publishing journey.

When I first decided to write a book about self-publishing, the first thing I did was outline it, and I made an announcement via Facebook. That was almost a year ago. Before a few months ago, I wasn't sure if this book would come to life, and I wasn't sure that I could pull it off. Well, I left all the negative thinking behind, and I thought about the daily questions or Facebook inbox messages I would receive asking me how I did it, or basically asking me for help with the process. A lot of "where to start" questions.
I had to write this book for the content creators who are looking to create another stream of income, people who are dedicated to helping others and creating a passive cash flow. I wanted to help and educate them on self-publishing the

content that they already provide on their YouTube channels or blog, and convert it into successful e-books or paperbacks.

I now understand that this process has taught me so much, and I love giving advice with a little comedy on the side. Giving you the real run down and all the pros and cons of various topics when it comes to self-publishing is what I wanted to accomplish, and having your worksheets and checklists to help you make sure every detail is correct when it comes to publishing your book.

Following my advice will be a stepping stone for you to create your own book. One thing I do know is that creativity is a gift, and you should use your gift to give to others. I hope throughout reading this that you are able to stop and put every advice into play after each chapter. I want this step-by-step guide to help you become a future best-seller. My hopes are that once you are done self-publishing your book, you will pass this title along to more people just like you, so they can learn how to be successful in the publishing world.

I want to take a look back on the different chapters and topics we talked about in this book, offering my very last words to you so that you go with all the confidence you had as soon as you picked up this book. The stress of completing and publishing your work will scare you and it's okay to be afraid. I am here to reassure you that this is the right choice, and if you ponder on the idea of your finished product too long, you'll just continue to talk yourself out of residual income. No one should ever pass up on their dreams or income.

At the beginning of the book, I was able to take you through the steps of Finding Your Passion; this is pretty much like defining your niche. If you're a blogger, you pretty much have this down pack, and your blog is targeted towards a certain topic. As a writer who wants to publish novels, you never really have to narrow down your genre. Never let anyone put you in a box when it comes to your writing style. Always push the envelope and strive to be greater than the last writer.

What I'm about to say about creating original content is imperative: never fall victim to being a copycat. There will be inspiration all around you, and copy for websites and content is becoming a big part of this industry. Never let anyone's work flow into your own. Being a copycat is a short-lived career. I challenge you to think outside the box and push to break barriers in every genre you decide to write in.

Once you narrow down your book topic, outlining it should be fun. This might be when the voices start to come out in full force; plots or topics come to you in the shower or when you're checking out at the grocery store. Random pictures you see can spark a whole new story. That's talent—you got this. Bring the book closer to your ears, I have a few words that need to jump from the pages.: now real talent is writing a book without an outline and staying on topic. You, my friend, have a gift.

Whether your book title and cover comes first or last, it should involve rounds of testing and research. There are so many tools nowadays; you can create polls and have readers or your peers vote. It's always good to have a "no" man or woman on your team who can be honest with you. This shouldn't be a negative thing, but it should be your go-to person who is able to be open and frank with you. If you're able to have two people like this in your life who are total opposites, I'd say you're very fortunate. Again, it's always your choice, and their opinions are only to help you succeed.

If you have at least three chapters ready and you have an outline, this is when you need to start forming your beta team of readers and researching for an editor who can meet your needs and who you work well with. This process shouldn't be stressful. This will be one of those connection type business relationships. Either they get it, or they don't. You have the option to say, this won't work, or, you are perfect for the job. Never feel like you must settle because someone was referred to you, either. You should build your own team based on your experience alone.

The best part of your campaign will be marketing. You must learn to be a genius and very innovative when it comes to marketing. I love Canva (www.canva.com) for graphics and creating infographics that are parallel to my book. Marketing sometimes should be simple, and fun. You should have your brand colors, and your fonts picked out to make everything cohesive. Canva's business platform, Canva for Work is impressive for a small fee. Again, never pay for something that you're not ready for. There are numerous free services around that you can use until you are making enough to have real expenses.

Book formatting is crucial to me; the way your book looks on Microsoft Word, as a .pdf, or on an Excel sheet, nine times out of ten is how it will look in print. I love looking at the structure of my favorite books and even studying books in my genre about the same topic to see what their formatting looks like. Also look at the top five or ten best-sellers to see what stands out about the format for you. Those are the same qualities you want to have in your book. But again, tailor it to your liking and your book's needs.

I've been able to give you in-depth information about different services for your self-publishing needs, and no matter what route you choose, it's because it was the best service for you. No matter how much information and tips I can give you, you should always research some more. Information changes, but the core of each system usually stays the same year after year. So whether you use KDP Select, CreateSpace, IngramSpark, vanity publishing, or hybrid publishing, you will be successful, no doubt.

I have so much faith in my aspiring writers and content creators who successfully complete this book. I know you will go on to do great things with this information and surpass any goals that I have set in my mind for you.
Take this book and keep it close throughout your writing journey. Use every tool and repeat it as many times as necessary. My ultimate goal here is to always inspire everyone to live their dreams.

// Acknowledgements

I'd like to say thank you to:

My Hubbub Shawn Smith for helping me with my goals for this book. Thank you for the long talks and for your daily wisdom.

Mango Publishing, for giving me the opportunity to create a book that I have dreamed of for the past year.

Hugo my editor, who has been with me every step of the way on this journey.

Thanks Joshua, and Michelle for keeping me on track leading up to the release.

// About the Author

Cinquanta C. Cox-Smith is a National Bestselling author, content creator, and veteran. Cinquanta has been featured in Georgetown Times, Everything Girls Love, and numerous radio shows on WDJY 99.1 FM.

She is a hardworking entrepreneur; her breakout series, Journeys of the Heart, has captured the hearts of many readers. Each of Cinquanta's novels in this series have dealt with very real issues. Journeys of The Heart dealt with rape, work-life balance, and love; New Birth & New Life explored life after prison, family businesses, and parenting; and Life of a Star: Before the Fame examined dysfunctional families, friendships, drugs and alcohol. In Cox-Smith's upcoming release, Battle My Love, she will delve into deployment, dual military, and blended families.

Cox-Smith is originally from Georgetown, South Carolina. She resides in Fort Riley, Kansas, with her husband Shawn and two kids, Kyree and Sharye Smith.

CPSIA information can be obtained
at www.ICGtesting.com
Printed in the USA
BVOW08s2345010517

482887BV00003B/6/P